Writing scientific papers and giving talks at meetings and conferences are essential parts of research scientists' work, and this short, straightforwardly written book will help workers in all scientific disciplines to present their results effectively. The first chapter is about writing a scientific paper and is a revision of an essay that won first prize in a competition organized by Koch–Light some years ago. Later chapters discuss the preparation of manuscripts, speaking at meetings and writing theses. One chapter is for scientists whose first language is not English. Another is addressed to those in North America. The last chapter gives information about dictionaries, style books and other literature.

COMMUNICATING IN SCIENCE
Writing a scientific paper and
speaking at scientific meetings

COMMUNICATING IN SCIENCE
Writing a scientific paper and speaking at scientific meetings

Second edition

VERNON BOOTH
Formerly of Trinity College, Cambridge

CAMBRIDGE
UNIVERSITY PRESS

Published by the Press Syndicate of the University of Cambridge
The Pitt Building, Trumpington Street, Cambridge CB2 1RP
40 West 20th Street, New York, NY 10011–4211, USA
10 Stamford Road, Oakleigh, Melbourne 3166, Australia

First published 1984
Second edition 1993
Reprinted 1993

Printed in Great Britain at the University Press, Cambridge

A catalogue record for this book is available from the British Library

Library of Congress cataloguing in publication data

Booth, Vernon.
Communicating in science : writing a scientific paper and speaking at scientific meetings /
Vernon Booth. – 2nd ed.
    p.   cm.
Includes bibliographical references and index.
ISBN 0–521–42915–3 (pbk.)
1. Communication in science.   2. Lectures and lecturing.
3. Technical writing.   I. Title.
Q223.B664   1993
808′.0665–dc20   92–37481 CIP

ISBN 0 521 42915 3   paperback
(ISBN 0 521 27771 X   first edition)

CE

Dedicated to T. W. Fline

Contents

Foreword

This final edition of 'Communicating' was assembled by Cambridge University Press from material prepared by Vernon Booth before his death in 1991. His family would like to thank the Press for thus making publication possible.

Balloons & instructions for
the typist & the printer

Don't
type
these

tail

it

[Fig. 4
near
here]

[Gk
alpha]

Entries in the margin that are ringed
are said to be in a 'balloon'. If
the balloon has a ⅄ and a caret, the
word(s) go into the text. If there is
no tail, the balloon *either* contains
clarification of blurred words, or it
contains instructions. If the instructions
are for the printer they may be typed
and bounded by two [] rather than
enclosed in a ring.

　　To remove a word, cross it out
boldly. to remove a small character,
draw a tiny wiggle.

　　If you have crossed out a piece,
then wish it to be kept, under line it

stet

with Dots ~~and~~ write 'stet' in the margin.
Stet means let it stand.

□ ~~There~~ *is* no guarantee ⅄ given that these
~~these~~ conventions are accepted or under-

NP

stood everywhere. Indicate that a
new paragraph (NP) is needed as
shown.

run on

　　If no NP is needed, draw
a snake and write 'run on'.

Explanation for the second edition

In one laboratory in Cambridge, if a person became unapproachable, we said he or she was giving birth. Paper labour can be a traumatic experience, but should not be. The writing of a paper, or a book, although indeed a task, should be a pleasant occupation. Books on scientific writing have been published, but scientists 'do not have time' to read them. So, in 1970, I wrote an essay, *Writing a Scientific Paper*, and submitted it for a competition organized by Koch–Light Ltd; the essay was awarded first prize, and issued as a booklet.

Later editions of the booklet grew longer and were published by the Biochemical Society. For the CUP version, various sections were expanded into chapters. This made the book longer, but the principal chapter remained short and kept its original title. The subtitle of the previous CUP edition was *writing and speaking*. This was felt to be misleading; so it has been changed. Numerous other changes have been made for this edition.

Chapters One and Two are intended primarily to help scientists, engineers and others to write papers for journals and to give short talks. However, nearly all the suggestions also apply to the writing of books and the delivery of full lectures.

The style, especially of the first chapter, is succinct, at times even terse. So much had to be written, in so small a space, that conciseness was highly desirable. Chapter One is not suitable for fast reading.

Parts of the book are written in the imperative, the simplest style. This is not intended to be categorical. True, certain parts are controversial; but life would be dull if we all agreed. There may be errors; most books have errors. But I ask you to read it (as an examinee once added) E. & O.E. (errors and omissions excepted).

Some of the words that are discussed are in 'quotes' or *italic*. A plethora of quotes and italic can be irritating; so, where the meaning should be clear without them, they are not used, even at the risk of some loss of consistency.

Examples of a directive being discussed are referred to in brackets. Thus [**1** (10)] means there is an illustrative example or more information in the line marked (10) in the margin of Chapter One.

You will see T. W. Fline mentioned in various places. This refers to **T**hose **W**hose **F**irst **L**anguage **I**s **N**ot **E**nglish. Whenever we write or speak, we must think of these people.

The majority of papers submitted for publication are returned to authors for revision. Naturally, you would like each of your papers to be accepted without change. This book cannot guarantee your fulfilling that ambition, but perhaps it will help.

As you read this book, you may realize that I enjoyed writing it. I offer best wishes that you too will enjoy writing, preparing scripts and speaking.

I am grateful to many, many colleagues, as well as to several editors at CUP and in various countries, for help and suggestions.

Vernon Booth
January 1991

Glossary of some printers' terms

balloon. Ring drawn round instructions to the printer. [Page 46.]

bold. Heavy type **as here**. In a script, underline with a wavy line.

braces. Curly brackets { }.

brackets. Square brackets [ ]. The term bracket is used in a general way
to include **parentheses** ( ), **braces** { } and angle brackets ⟨ ⟩. To an
author brackets usually mean parentheses.

caps, upper case. CAPITAL LETTERS. In a script underline
three times.

copy. The script. To avoid confusion, a **photocopy** should be so named.

em rule. Long dash (—). Length of cap M. [**1** (33).] Many publishers
use a spaced en rule (–).

en rule. Short dash (–). Half the length of em rule. [Page 21.]

foliation. Numbering of folios.

folio. (1) Sheet of script. (2) Page number. (3) Sheet of paper of any
size folded once.

full point. Full stop, period.

index. (1) Alphabetical list of topics at the end of a book. Plural,
indexes. (2) See **superior** below.

inferior, subscript. Small low digit(s) or other character(s). $H_2SO_{4,\ 2n}$.

ital, italic. *Sloping type*. Spelt with lower-case 'i'. In a script, underline
once.

justified lines. Lines of print made the same length by varying the
spaces between words. See **window** below.

leading. Space between lines of type. Pronounced 'ledding'.

l.c., lower case. Small letters, i.e. not caps.

legend, caption. Explanation to a figure. Term occasionally also used
for explanation to a table. Ideally, legends should be understandable
without reference to the text, and, to identify them they are often set in
smaller type. Legends (or captions) to figures are usually placed below,

whereas those for tables are usually placed, more logically, above the display.

letter space. Space b e t w e e n letters.

numeral. Digit. See page 16 under Homonyms.

par. Paragraph. [**1** (16).] **N.P.** New paragraph. [Page xii.] Indicate NP by □ or ⌐ .

parens. Parentheses, round brackets ( ). [**1** (18).]

quotes are often called 'inverted commas' though only the first is that; the second is an apostrophe or raised comma; 'single', "double".

reference marks. * † ‡ § ‖ ¶ ** †† . . . . Use them in this order for footnotes.

reprint, offprint. A printed copy of a single article from a journal or book. If available before publication then known as a **preprint**.

rom, roman. Normal upright type, not italic or bold. Spelt with lower-case 'r'.

run on. Continue in same para. See last sentence, page xii.

sanserif, sans. Type without serifs. THIS is sans. H girder; O ring; S shape; T join; U tube; V groove. For text, sans is less legible than type with serifs. [**8** (1).] See The typewriter's or word processor's type face (page 47).

sm. cap, small caps. Capital-style letters only slightly larger than l.c. Used for EMPHASIS, for HEADINGS and for some CONVENTIONS. In a script line, underline twice.

superior, superscript. Small high digit(s) or other character(s). mm^3, ^{2n}. Also called **index**; plural, indices.

widow or **club line.** Short line at the top of a page.

window. Wide,   ugly   gap   between   words   in a   line.

word space. Space between words.

Chapter One
Writing a scientific paper

Before you write

Here are four suggestions about what you might do before writing a paper.

1. If notebooks are used, good notebook discipline is helpful. When an experiment is finished, try to record your conclusion in words, together with your findings and on the same page. Make tables. Draw graphs and stick them into the book. Keep a file in which to record summaries of results from many experiments, and group them by subject. Some experiments will each provide results for various summaries. Number each book and each right-hand page. Then, even after some years, an experiment can be found from the file as e.g. 9;43 (book 9; p. 43). Write the date at the top of the page.

Prompt recording of a summary for each experiment compels you to give critical thought to the experiment at the best time, and may move you to repeat a control test while you still have the materials. Clark (1960) makes an eloquent appeal for keeping adequate notes. Write every digit unmistakably. Think: 'I must so write my notes that another person can read them if I am ill, or worse'. Then you should understand them yourself when you come to write the paper.

2. *Speaking makes you think out arguments*; and listeners' criticisms
(1) may prevent your publishing a clanger. Some institutes operate a regular tea club or occasional seminar at which researchers tell colleagues about their work. If your institute has no club, or the programme is filled, invite colleagues to your room to listen to you. Display diagrams. If you have no projector, use a felt-tip pen to draw diagrams and tables on the back of a roll of wallpaper. Hang the paper over a chair on the bench. Do – speak – slowly.
(2) Nothing clarifies ideas in one's mind so much as explaining them to other people.

I

3. The third suggested pre-writing activity is based on Woodford's (**8** (3)) 'reservoirs'. Take 8 sheets of paper. Boldly label them

Title Summary Intro Mat Meth Results Disc Ref

Write ideas for your paper, whenever they come to you, as notes on the appropriate sheets (reservoirs). Use differently coloured sheets if possible. Carry a card everywhere – even to bed. Jot down ideas as they occur. Transfer the notes to the reservoirs and put a fresh card in your pocket or handbag. Rewrite a cluttered reservoir from time to time; if you wait too long, you may forget what some of your notes meant. Hold the reservoirs in a clothes peg (pin), not in a wire clip which may catch on other papers.

Some writers construct a skeleton, an outline scheme, before they start to write. Should you do this it is still advisable first to prepare the reservoirs. In particular, a skeleton for the Discussion may help you to muster your ideas in the best order and to avoid repetition.

4. Prepare tables and figures.

Honesty & accident

If the result of an experiment seems 'wrong', record it none the less, and watch for a repeat. Many a discovery has been made by accident: serendipity is alive and productive. However, people have been known to manipulate or 'doctor' their 'wrong' results. Manipulators may have regrets later.

When to begin writing

(3) My research supervisor said 'Writing a paper is as important as experiments. Is it unreasonable, then, if it takes as long?' Oft-repeated advice is 'Set aside your paper for some weeks, then read it. You may be amazed at what you wrote.' You may even discover a passage you yourself cannot understand. If you follow this advice, and believe that supervisor, you must start writing early. Writing as the work proceeds reveals gaps in knowledge, gaps that should be filled while laboratory facilities are still available.

Arrangement of a scientific paper

The commonest arrangement for a research paper is that indicated by the order of the reservoirs mentioned above. Some investigations are suitable for results and discussion to be written together in narrative form. If you use this form, write your Conclusion as a separate section.

Where to start

Even though you have enough material, you may have postponed
writing a projected paper. Perhaps you find it difficult to start. I do.
You do not have to begin with the Introduction. Begin with the easiest
section. This may be Methods, for you should know what you did. Use
the 'reservoirs', and cross out the notes as you consume them.

Next, perhaps, you might start on the Results. Write the first draft
'in your own words' just as though you are telling a friend about your
discoveries. Don't worry – yet – about grammar, aptest words & style.
The immediate objective is to get going. You can polish the style later.
This paragraph was so written, and the needless words and hackneyed
phrases have not yet been polished out.

The Conclusion of a paper is so important that you should make its
first draft in time to allow for re-draftings.

Stocktaking

Now take stock. The outline is complete, diagrams and tables are
ready, the Discussion is planned, the Conclusion is drafted and
Methods are written. Oh joy! the paper is half finished. A happy
author writes better than a worried one.

Title & key words

Some searchers may read only a paper's Title and Summary. So both
are supremely important parts. Compose trial versions of the title as
early in your writing as you can; re-examine them later.

On your first reservoir sheet write key words for the Title. Let the
Title's first word be a key word if possible; in lists of titles such a word
is better than 'The'. Remove other waste words such as 'on', 'study',
'investigation' . . . . The Title should be short yet specific, not general:
a reader, attracted by a title, may be disappointed to find that the
paper is about only one specialized aspect of the subject promised.
Have you experienced such a disappointment?

Many journals require a Headline or Running title as well as the
Title. An ingenious paraphrase of the Title can supplement the latter.
For example, the Latin name of a species might appear in the Title and
the common name in the Running title.

If the journal needs key words, you can provide them from your
reservoir.

Summary

If the editor permits, compose the Summary in numbered paragraphs. The first should state – briefly – what you did. Then come the main results. Lists of values may be indigestible for your readers; so use words, supplemented by a few key values. State your conclusion in the last paragraph. If you have no succinct conclusion, you might write 'The effect of A upon B is discussed'.

(4)   If a summary is long, readers may look only at the first and last paragraphs. Although a well-written summary may be lifted by abstractors, a long summary will be shortened, perhaps by the omission of what you consider vital parts.

Write the Summary in the past tense, except perhaps the last paragraph.

Some journals print the Summary in small type. How odd!

Introduction to a paper

The Introduction should state the problem, and perhaps ask a question. The objective must be clear. If you modified your objective after you began the work, give the current version. Do you still think you asked the right question?

The quoting of numerous papers in the Introduction is no longer good practice. [If much has been published, and you think it warrants a review, write that separately and submit it to an editor.] Refer to papers that, taken together, show that a problem exists. If another paper gives many references, refer to that. However, beware of lifting references – from that paper – together with misquotations of information from the original papers. That has been done . . . . For example, one abstractor supposed that *Kaninchen* meant little dog; and Yamane's work on the rabbit [*Kaninchen* means rabbit] has gone into the literature as being on the dog. For this and other cautionary tales, see Hartree (1976). Roland (1976) reports that J. Hlava, a Czech, wrote an article 'On dysentery' and added a Czech translation of the title: 'O. Uplavici'. An abstractor cited the author as O. Uplavici; so an author who never lived went into the literature for 50 years.

In the last sentence of the Introduction, it is accepted practice to state the conclusion. A reader can better appreciate the evidence that follows if it is clear what conclusion is being supported. However, this version of the conclusion must be brief. Some authors repeat much of the Summary in the Introduction. That is not an acceptable practice.

Materials & Methods

If the description of materials is short it may be included in Methods. Avoid trade names if practicable, not to avoid advertising, but because they may not be understood abroad. [Do you know what Klampits or Barbistors are? or what Skellysolve means?] If you use a local name for polymethylmethacrylate or other compound, give the chemical name at first mention of the trade name.

Write what you did in operational order. Invert 'The urn was dated after restructuring' to 'The urn was reconstructed, then dated'. You should so describe the methods you used that others can repeat the experiments. You must be concise, yet you must not omit essential detail. If you used 'alcohol' say which alcohol. If you controlled, or even measured, the humidity and ventilation in an animal room, say so: they may be nearly as important as temperature. If you centrifuged a suspension, say whether supernatant or pellet was used for the next operation. Similarly, if you filtered a suspension, say which part was retained; it has not always been easy for a reader to conjecture.

If you used control experiments, permit no doubt about their nature. The reader may not be able to guess what you omitted for each control.

If your paper is about a new method, ask a visitor or a technician to test your description by applying the method in your absence. The result of the omission of one detail can be illuminating.

Results

Before you write about your Results it may be advisable to study Units and quantities (p. 25) and Tables (p. 24).

Replicate observations should not usually be given. Instead, offer the mean and a measure of the variability if you can. The range is not satisfactory; if there are enough replicates for the range to be of use then there are enough for estimating the standard deviation (s.d.) of one observation, the standard error of the mean (s.e.m.) or the coefficient of variation (c.v.). Give the number of observations or the degrees of freedom within parentheses: $12.65 \pm 0.22 \ (n = 12)$. Perhaps you can make a pooled estimate of the variance (or other statistic) from the whole study. You can then give individual uncluttered values.

Journals ask for tables and figures to be clear without reference to the text. This requires concise explanation in legends, an explanation of abbreviations, and care in the avoidance of repetition in the text and in other legends, as well as consistency between text and legends.

Discussion

The Discussion must not be so long as to deter a reader, yet it must contain logical argument. Do not repeat descriptions of other people's findings if they are in the Introduction; refer to that. Avoid summarizing your results in the Discussion. Mention them, take them as read or refer to a table or even to the Summary (quote a paragraph number, if used). Enlarge upon the significance of your new results and explain how they add to existing knowledge. You may have formulated your problem as a question in the Introduction. If you can now give the answer, that facilitates discussion.

Think critically, not only about other people's work but about your own. For example, ask yourself 'Can my hypothesis be refuted? Can my results have another explanation?' Maier (1933) told the students in one of two large groups that, were they unable to solve the problem given to them, they should try to ignore their first approach and seek an altogether different line. (The other group, the control, was not told.) This worked – in the 'told' group a larger proportion solved the problem than in the control group – yet it is difficult to achieve such 'lateral thinking', as de Bono (1967) calls the modern development. The following example shows how important is such 'no-prejudice rethinking'. Two authors published graphs to prove their thesis that xanthine oxidase and the Schardinger enzyme (aldehyde oxidase) are distinct enzymes. Later, their graphs were used by another author to confirm the opposite (now accepted) view that the enzymes are identical. Had those first authors given their results more thought, they too might have reversed their conclusion. The literature contains abundant examples of inconclusive thinking. Writers should take care not to add to them by publishing in haste.

W. Pauli wrote 'I don't mind your thinking slowly: I mind your publishing faster than you can think.' [Translated by Mackay (1977).]

Conclusion

If you are fortunate, your Message (or part of it) may survive in textbooks – although you may not be given a whole sentence! So the Conclusion needs precise wording. Your Conclusion may appear three times: in the Discussion, the Summary and the Introduction. Do not repeat the wording; paraphrase it. If the reader has not understood one version, another may help. Use the shortest version for the Summary.

Parting remarks. Perhaps you have not yet reached a conclusion, but have contributed towards one. You may like to end with 'Parting remarks'. Make them short, but do not bring 'final' into the heading. One paper concluded with 'We admit we have raised more questions than we have solved.'

References, Bibliography or Literature cited

Write each reference on a card. Arrange the cards in order and give them to the typist at the final typing of your paper when you have checked them against your revised text. This scheme leads to fewer errors than does retyping the references at every retyping of the paper, although the advent of word processors has made 'editing' the References a much easier job. Each journal arranges references in a particular style, which should be followed. Give the typist a copy of the journal to provide an example of style. If references in the text are made by superior digits, avoid 'the value was 24^2'; change to 'the value was 24 (ref. 2)'.

Check the typed list against the original papers. Also check that the spelling of names in text and Bibliography agree. Errors are *very* common in papers submitted to editors. (See Numbering, p. 48.)

(6)

Written English

Good written English is nearly the same as good spoken English. Grandiloquence has no place in scientific writing. We need to convey ideas effectively, to make it easy for the reader to understand what we write, not to exhibit our vocabulary. Indeed, those who use pompous language may even be suspected of having nothing important to say! Try to envisage the reader; write in a manner not too technical, not too elementary. Write as though you are talking to a reader, relating your experiments, but restrain colloquialisms.

Clear English. Ask yourself often: would T. W. Fline [p. xiv] understand what I write? Write short sentences, but not all of them so short as to produce a staccato effect. Cure a staccato passage by linking two sentences (as I have done here with a 'but'), but do this only seldom, so as to keep to 'one idea per sentence' with occasional exceptions. A satisfying sentence has two main verbs (Perttunen, 1975).

If you train yourself to speak well, that will help you to develop a good written style. In conversation, choose words with care, speak deliberately and clearly.

Grammar

English grammar is simpler than that of many languages, yet some writers are careless about the small amount that does exist. People abroad who learn English as a foreign language mostly learn it grammatically because they are used to complex grammar in their own languages. So when they meet doubtful grammar in a published work, or at a conference, they may be confused. On their behalf, I appeal to you to persuade emergent authors to follow rules of grammar and to punctuate carefully.

In English, the same word can sometimes be used as a noun (*tin*), an adjective (*tin* can) and a verb (to *tin* the copper wire). Indeed, almost any noun may be 'verbed' and any adjective 'nouned': medical, high, sabbatical. But this freedom is needlessly abused. Consider the phrase 'the book was authored'. Why not say 'written'? 'Authored' gives no special shade of meaning. Where a verb is needed but none exists, it is practical to use a noun (to program, to chromatograph); but 'to gift' (mineral samples were gifted by Dr Fob) is unnecessary.

Mutual editing

In courses on rapid reading, one is told not to go back to re-read a passage. A trained reader may not return to a sentence whose meaning was not grasped. How can you discover such passages in your own writing? One way is to put the paper away for a month, then read it afresh. This may be impractical. Another is to have colleagues read your paper. Ask them both to make general comments and to mark every sentence they had to read twice. If they are critical, thank them nevertheless, for, if they fail to understand you, others might fail too and your Message will be lost.

For nearly 2000 years it has been known that we see other people's faults more easily than our own. (Parable of the mote and beam, Matthew 7, iii.) Moreover, it is fun to cross out needless words in other people's papers. Therefore, make a deal with your colleagues; if they will let you 'correct' their papers, you will let them correct yours. Do not use red ink, which is offensive to some; green is more soothing.

You may have noted a repetition above. That is deliberate, because emphasis is needed. Hundreds of the errors I have seen, in papers that had already been accepted but not yet edited, ought to have been seen by a critical colleague and then corrected – before submission.

However senior you be, ignore the 'statuskline', or hierarchy, and ask for constructive criticism, not flattery, from your juniors. Such editing should be good training for them.

Literary style

(7)   *Noun adjectives.* In English, nouns may be used as adjectives; that is, as modifiers of a true noun. One might write 'an oil engine needs engine oil' or 'glass bottles are made of bottle glass'. But the use of nouns as adjectives may lead to confusion unless made with care. For such terms as 'dog meat' or 'cat fish' make it clear which of the two meanings is intended. 'Rapid gas apparatus deterioration' is better written as 'Rapid deterioration of gas apparatus', and 'product treatment' as 'treatment of the product'. Even the simple 'drug dose' seems clumsy. If you dislike recurrent 'of', the occasional genitive case may be used.

There is no suggestion here that nouns should never be used adjectivally. Many are so used satisfactorily, including hydrogen bond, gold size, oak tree, steel plate, SI units.

Take care to avoid confusion. *We* may know that a spring washer is a sprung washer, not a machine for washing springs, but would T. W. Fline know that? And would the title 'Cancer in rubber workers' be understood?

When two or more nouns are used as adjectives of one noun, the phrase may become inelegant. Consider the following: isotope dilution assay results; pH 6.8 phosphate buffer; multiple conductor galvanized angle steel pylon system; we devised a new short chain fluorocarbon aerosol can valve. Such phrases are difficult to comprehend; the reader finds that each successive noun is not the real noun; words have to be stored mentally until the substantive being modified is reached. Therefore, avoid long adjectival phrases, or stacked modifiers as Woodford (**8** (3)) calls them (see also p. 54). Even if the modifier contains no noun adjective, it may be troublesome, as this example shows: a frequently heated and therefore deeply coloured viscous solution . . . . The use of hyphens may lead to improvement of some phrases, but rewriting is usually best.

Note that *in vivo*, *excess* and *de novo* are not adjectives, but that *subliminal*, *optimal*, *minimal* and *maximal* are. Write 'test *in vitro*' not *in vitro* test. People would not write 'in glass test'.

Comparatives. A passage that contains a comparative sometimes causes difficulty: what does 'lions eat more than antelopes' mean? Make clear what is more than what, and only compare things that are comparable. Instead of 'starch yielded more glucose than maltose' write either '. . . than did maltose' or 'starch produced a greater yield of glucose than of maltose'. Do not omit 'those in' from 'bearings in steam engines lasted longer than those in diesel engines'.

Wrongly attached participle. A verb in the active voice needs a subject, an operator, either actual or understood. One of the most common errors submitted for publication is exemplified by 'having completed the observations the telescope . . .' or 'a bend was observed in the bridge using a strain gauge'. Was the bridge really using a gauge? Phrases such as the following make people laugh. After standing in boiling water for 2 h, examine the flask; electronic devices should be made safe before leaving the laboratory; and goggles are required to do the experiment. Yet such errors (aberrations, faults, lapses . . .) are often submitted to editors. Read what Fowler [8 (9)] or the authors of style books listed in Chapter Eight have written on Unattached, Wrongly attached or Dangling participles and infinitives.

Gerund. A participle may become a kind of noun (called a gerund), as in 'Writing a paper'. If the adding of 'the' and 'of' (e.g. before and after 'adding' in this sentence) makes grammatical sense, the -ing word is a gerund. Applying this test, you can see that 'Using a dynamometer, the tractive effort was measured' is not allowable because 'Using' is a wrongly attached verb here, not a gerund, being wrongly attached to 'effort'. Change the sentence to 'Using a dynamometer, we measured . . .' or to 'A dynamometer was used for measuring the tractive . . .' or add 'By' → 'by using a . . .'. In 'Applying this test, you . . .' (see 6 lines above) the 'you' was the subject, and the phrase is allowable.

Be alert for dangling verbs. So many sentences start with 'Judging by' or 'Based on' that these participles are becoming accepted for use in that way.
Even so, let other words that end in -ing or -ed warn you to ensure that each is either a gerund or is properly attached to an operator.

Using is written and spoken so often without an expressed operator that it may eventually become a preposition (compare *providing*). Even if you accept that event, you will be wise to ensure that the operator is always clearly understood. The phrase 'He could not stop the mill using the brake' should not be written because it has two meanings. Add 'by' before 'using'.

Schoenfeld [8 (7)] writes typically amusing pieces on *using*.

Waffle, needless words

(8)
(9)

If you put aside your draft, and then examine it later, this is the time to expunge what Houp & Pearsall [8 (4)] call 'empty words'. Such phrases as 'It is worth pointing out in this context that' may be deleted without affecting the sense. So may the following.

It is significant to note the fact that
relevant to mention here that results
reported here demonstrate that
It is known that
It should be borne in mind in this connection that
found to be

Such phrases, which correspond to spoken *anderms*, are not needed in reports. Many phrases may be shortened. For 'It is plainly demonstrable from the curves presented in Fig. 2' write 'Fig. 2 shows'. If a piece is introduced by 'Needless to say', why say it? 'Recent' is usually superfluous if the date is given in the references. Usually 'we wish to thank' means 'we thank', 'has been shown to be' means 'is', and 'proved to be' means 'were'. 'It can be seen in Table 4 that' may be omitted and '(Table 4)' placed after the statement. 'Because of the fact that' may be cut to 'because'; 'concerning' may be replaced by 'on', 'therefore' and 'consequently' by 'so'. Indeed, *so* is a neglected word.

The following phrases may each be cut to one word:

actual truth	as to whether	weather conditions
all of	completely full	would appear
both of	definitely proved	absolute minimum
half of	exactly true	in an exhausted condition
quite unique	first of all	lose out on
very similar	red in colour	large in size
join together	round in shape	significant finding

As Strunk (8 (10)) writes, MAKE EVERY WORD COUNT.

Double hedging. Avoid repetition of the type 'may be probable', 'seems that . . . could be possible' and 'is supposed it might . . . in some cases'. Such hedging weakens discussion. If a writer is so unsure that hedging is felt to be necessary, is he or she really ready to publish?

One possibility seems to be that triple hedging may produce flabby writing, as it has done in this sentence. If a hedging is later either proved *or* disproved the early author can claim original mention, but will not be admired for that.

(10) *Pronouns.* When you write *it*, *this*, *which* or *they*, are you sure the meaning is plain? Readers may be unwilling to search back for the meaning of 'it'. A pronoun deputizes (usually) for the nearest previous noun of the same number (singular or plural). If you have used a pronoun for a more distant noun, perhaps the noun should be repeated, as *Summary* is above [**1** (4)]. We may know what the author means by 'seeds were placed in petri dishes which were then softened in water'. However, if 'which' were to refer to something even more distant than 'seeds', we might not know.

A sentence that starts with 'It' should be examined critically. It may be that the sentence starts, as this one does, with an 'It' that does not refer to a previous noun, yet the reader momentarily expects it to do that. So, turn 'It is believed that carbon dating gives' . . .' to 'Carbon dating is believed to give . . .'. Two other arguments against the starting of a sentence with 'It' (needless words and distant references) have been explained above [**1** (9) (10)].

Personal pronoun. An occasional 'I' need not be shunned. Indeed, 'I' may be desirable to dispel doubt about who did something. If you quote published results and then give yours, claim the latter. 'The author' might seem to mean the other writer, not you. [See (11) below.] Never, of course, write 'we' for yourself, or use 'I' immodestly or too often.

Personal pronouns should not appear in a summary because they will make an abstractor's task difficult.

Tense, mood & voice

Authors usually write about their new work in the simple past tense: 'I saw sparks' or 'sparks were seen'. Do not describe your results in the compound past tense; write 'were' not 'have been'. Other people's work is variously reported. Many authors use the present tense; some use the compound past tense, as in 'Nob has studied fossils'. A change

(11) in tense helps us to distinguish between your work and his. Day [**8** (5)] explains why the present tense is desirable in the reporting of published work.

Working directions for a method are sometimes written in the imperative mood. This is done partly because it makes the most direct style.

The passive voice, commonly used to describe results, sometimes makes clumsy construction. Turn a passive phrase to direct style when you can. For example, turn 'oxygen is needed for combustion' to 'combustion needs oxygen'. 'It is reported by Job' is better written as 'Job reports'. 'Excavation was involved in the project' should be 'the project included excavation'. Sometimes a passive phrase may be avoided by writing 'I'.

Never 'subject a patient to examination': examine him or her.

Choice of words

Beware of using words whose true meaning is not what you wish to convey. Here are some words that deserve especial care.

case. I recommend that you read what Fowler, Partridge, Day or other authority (Chapter Eight) has written about *case*. A sloppy misuse is to make the word act as a pronoun – as in 'the above cases' – so that the reader has to go back to find what the cases were. I have met cases where I could not be sure to what the writer referred; did 'two cases' mean two experiments, two animals or two observations on one animal? Replace *case*, if you can, by a word that gives information, for example 'this mineral' or 'Expt 8'. Or shorten the phrase, as in these examples: in most c. (usually, mostly); in this c. (here); in all c. (always); in no c. (never); in that c. (so); in the c. of (for, in); was the c. (was true); the c. in question (this patient). 'In some c. this was the c.' needs no comment.

different is used too often. If two methods were used, *different* is not needed; if the methods were not different there would not be two. In '. . . applied different torsions' replace different by various. From '4 different kinds' omit 'different'.

due to and **owing to**. *Due to* often occurs where *owing to* would be better. *Due to* has the sense of caused by; *owing to* has the sense of because of. We may write 'the colour of the diamond was due to impurities' but 'owing to impurities the diamond was coloured'. If 'Due to' starts a sentence, that is probably wrong. Consider the sentence: 'Cardiac disease due to the use of drugs is not always fatal'. This implies that the disease is caused by drugs. If *due to* be replaced by *owing to*, we have the opposite meaning: the disease is not always fatal, because drugs are used. Commas make the meaning clear: 'Cardiac disease, owing to the use of drugs, is not always fatal'.

Must we lose *owing to* owing to careless substitution by *due to*?

efficient describes processes whose efficiency can be measured. A writer may mean effective. You may have devised a shaking machine or a warning device. Can you determine that it is efficient? A potentiometer-type power pack (for supplying desired voltages) was described as 'efficient'. Engineers who read that such apparatus is efficient, which it cannot be, may doubt the truth of other statements in the paper.

fact. When you write *fact*, do you truly mean undisputed knowledge? Effect, hypothesis, observation, value, result, phenomenon or finding may be more modest. 'These facts' may even be changed to words that give information, for example 'these similarities'. 'Due to the fact that' is better written as 'Because'. 'In spite of the fact that my results were negative' is bettered on several counts by 'Despite my finding no effect'. Strunk (**8** (10)) says, 'the fact that' should be revised out of every sentence in which it occurs. Careful writers do not describe their findings as facts. A 'fact' reported by an author may be contraindicated by results from another. This often happens.

flammable is preferred to inflammable. People sometimes take the latter to mean it will not burn. The sequel could be disastrous.

minimal means lowest, smallest, and should not be written for small.

parameter is sometimes used unwisely. Variable might be safer.

varying means changing. The word is often used wrongly in place of variable, varied or various. [**1** (20).] Computations made with varying formulas would have only little value, whereas those made with various formulas might confirm one another.

washable. Does *washable ink* mean resistant to washing, or removable?

which and **that**. If you are unsure about these words, recall the rule 'which describes, that defines'. Consider the phrases:

brown hens, which lay brown eggs, have yellow . . .
brown hens that lay brown eggs have yellow . . .

The first implies that brown hens lay brown eggs and also have the yellow character. The second means that those particular brown hens that lay brown eggs have it. Confirm your decision through the commas; if they are needed, write 'which'. Another example follows.

Pronouns that cannot easily be identified with nouns are said to dangle.

Dangling pronouns, which may be *it, ones or these*, are troublesome.

The first sentence *defines* the dangling pronoun and there are no commas. The second sentence *describes* pronouns as troublesome. Note the two commas, one before 'which', one before 'are' in the second sentence; if the parenthetic remark between them be omitted the sentence still makes sense: 'Dangling pronouns are troublesome'.

See also Homonyms, pp. 16 and 56.

Plain words. In general, use short rather than long words if they have the same meaning. Write:

about, not approximately, of the order of or *circa*;
use, not utilize or employ (employ implies payment; did you pay?)
have, not possess; enough, not sufficient;

Show may be better than demonstrate, disclose, exhibit or reveal. However, do not eschew (avoid, reject, disdain, spurn, scorn) a grand word if it conveys the meaning better than another: *syrup* is an aqueous solution that cannot be called watery; *expunge* is more vigorous than *remove* [**1** (9)]; *reveal* is apt in Chapter Seven (1).

When you write the first words in the following list do you mean the second, or vice versa? Brackets (parentheses); generally (usually); wire (cable); if (when, whether); plug (socket).

Mathematical terms are often used for non-mathematical meanings, which is undesirable if an ordinary word exists. For example, it is not advisable to write *centre* (a mathematical point) if you mean *middle*, or *degree* if you mean *extent*. For graphs, write *filled* symbol, not *solid*; and *unbroken* or *continuous*, not *solid*, line. In mathematics, an *area* has two dimensions, so use another word when you refer to more than a surface. In scientific writing, *negative* is best reserved for *minus* and for electric polarity; there are plenty of other words for *none*. 'No response' is more scientific than 'response was negative'.

Avoid the unscientific use of $\pm$ for *about* or for with and without (when $+$ or 0 is meant), and do not use equals ($=$) for *means*. *Certain* may sometimes be better than *positive*. Eight plus and $8 +$ are not so scientific as >8. (See also Chapter Four, pp. 47–8, on word processor type faces.)

Elegant variation. English abounds in near synonyms: different words that have almost the same meaning. Examples include begin, commence, start, launch, originate, initiate, auspicate. Repetition of a word within a sentence is considered to be bad style, which may be avoidable with synonyms. However, in scientific writing, a synonym should be used only if its meaning is clear. Repeat a word if the sense so requires. There may be a case for a synonym where a technical word might not be understood, but the writer must make it clear that the two words mean the same thing. At the first use, some authors write both words. [See The solidus, **1** (19).] Repetition may sometimes be avoided by the rewriting of a sentence. If a sentence has many *and*'s, try replacing one of them by *then*.

Homonyms. Many English words have more than one meaning. Where possible, use a word that has only one meaning. Never, in one passage, use the same word for different meanings, as for example in 'Factor *V* varied by a factor of 4' or 'For preservation one can can it'.

Normal has often been used as a trouble saver and has so many meanings that it should be avoided where possible. *Normal temperature* may mean 0 °C, 37.4 °C or 273 K. *Physiological saline* is more descriptive than *normal saline*. *Normal* should no longer be used to describe solutions. The accepted form is mol l^{-1}. Because mol l^{-1} is clumsy, is not an adjective and is unsuitable for speech, many people prefer M, mol/l or mol/L.

The use of existing words for new meanings causes confusion, especially to T. W. Fline. Chapter Six gives examples; here are others.

Cell is overworked; *cuvette* is better in spectrophotometry.

Reduce has various meanings. Avoid the word or clarify it.

Figure is used for picture, pattern, diagram, shape, number, digit or numeral, quantity or amount, price and value, as well as for calculate and even for think. The reservation of *figure* for the first meaning seems desirable. A number, such as 247, is composed of digits or numerals; 24.7 mg is a quantity; 2.47 in a table is a value. The abbreviation for ordinal 'Number' is 'no.'; cardinal 'number', used for quantities, should not be written 'no.'; write '. . . number of turns in coil no. 6 . . .'.

(13)

(14) *Foreign words.* If you use foreign words when English words will convey the meaning, you risk being accused of affectation. You also risk our failing to understand you because some of us do not know many foreign expressions. Sometimes the grammar is faulty. *Capita* is plural; hence, *per capita* means per heads. Did you realize that? Strictly, *media* is plural, but in modern usage has often become singular.

Conveyance of ideas without element of doubt

You may think this fuss over precision in the use of words 'is only cosmetic'. But, if you prefer not to take rules of grammar and usage seriously, may I plead as follows?

First, convey your Message clearly. Dixon [8 (12)] writes in a breezy style, yet his meaning is plain.

Secondly, do not be conservative about names. We have discarded vitriol, jar, fuming spirits of muriatic acid, candle power, probable error. So let us drop a.m. and p.m., formalin, glycerine, h.p., pet. ether, soda, carbolic. Is it fair to expect young people to learn archaic names as well as systematic terms?

Thirdly, please do not accelerate the demise of hitherto useful words. We have almost lost *very*, formerly a very useful word. Consider that last phrase: did the second *very* affect the meaning? The demise is hastened by such thoughtless uses as 'very unique' and 'very level'; yet on occasion we need the word. [1 (6).] *Surely*, *doubtless* and their synonyms no longer mean without doubt; 'no doubt' they will decline.

The meaning of *quite* is reversing: 'his method is quite good' now means less good than *good*. Other reversals include *release*, which formerly meant allow to go; now it is used for publish, that is push out, as in 'Provisional data release'. Philip Norman (1980) uses the term paranym for such opposites. In politics the use of paranyms is common, but scientists should not use them.

'Fig. 5 clearly shows' is common. Had *clearly* been omitted, a reader might believe the statement, but *clearly* alerts him, and the element of persuasion makes him sceptical. *Clearly* is becoming a paranym. 'Plainly visible in the figure' has the same effect.

I appeal to you to use words with care.

Good workmanship endures

After you are elected a Nobel laureate, people will look at your early papers. You may squirm with embarrassment if they discover that you once thought *accordance* meant accord or that '4 times more than' meant the same as 4 times as many as. [For argument, see Chapter Ex.] Scientists who look back at their early papers feel (justifiable) pleasure on finding good writing. I recommend you similarly to invest in the future.

You may think 'There are so many rules and pitfalls! How can I remember them all?' At first you cannot. But, if you persist, you will find that clear writing is a craft in which to take pleasure. The object of a writer should be to convey information with minimal effort from the reader. Although grammatical customs, like etiquette, are not all logically defensible, if you ignore them you may obscure your meaning.

Language in flux

English is changing. That is desirable to meet changing needs, but it is not desirable to lose meanings of useful words. When a new word is needed, it seems better to make one than to add to the plethora of homonyms by taking an existing word. An example of such invention is capacitor to replace condenser, which has other meanings. We need a word for s.e.m. – without the 'error' connotation. Another could be *andor* to avoid the algebraic *and/or*. But let us shun such horrors as *uniformization*.

Certain changed usages are common and may become established. Examples now occurring include: aliquot to mean *any* measured amount; a number were; these results suggest; ultraviolet light; under the circumstances; detergents and soap; restructured; significant not qualified by statistically; 100-volume H_2O_2; heighth; caustic, coronary, medical and other adjectives used as nouns. The first few examples may be acceptable. Others are not. No doubt you could add to the list, but do you find the trend agreeable?

Revision of the script must not be hurried

(15) A writer's work may become so familiar that the author may be bored when rereading it. The intense concentration needed for revision cannot be maintained for long. Therefore, I urge you to read only a few pages of script at a time, and to

READ THEM SLOWLY.

What you have written should make sense, not only as you read it, but when you read it aloud. Make it sound like intelligent conversation. Where you pause, insert a stop. Ask friends to read the script to you. Where they stumble, rewrite the passage.

Critical revision is more necessary than writers realize. Several of the books on writing that are listed in Chapter Eight contain errors and lapses in style. There may be some in this book, too. So, BE VIGILANT.

Let your aim be to make such people as myself redundant. The species is not yet endangered!

Extend your vigilance to repetition as well as to style and sense. In some papers the Introduction and the Discussion contain similar passages. In your script you may find parts of a method described in a legend or in notes to a table as well as in Results. Avoid such repetition if you can. If your Conclusion is repeated, as suggested elsewhere, paraphrase it. Other parts, the comprehension of which is paramount, may be said again differently, introduced perhaps by 'in other words'. Use this device sparingly, however, or you will be in trouble, and so shall I. For an example see **1** (3) with **1** (8), or **1** (1) and (2).

A great deal of needless repetition and verbiage is to be found, now as in the past, in so very many published papers, yet it may be that the authors were completely unaware of their unnecessary repetitions, a possibility that can be adduced as yet one more good reason that authors should have for asking a colleague both to read and to comment on their scientific writings. You may like to write out the previous sentence and, as you write, prune it to less than half. It can be done. Please do not spoil it for others by marking the print.

Spelling

Some words have alternative spellings. For example, show, gray, acknowledgement, disk, neutralize. If the choice is yours, use the spelling that better represents the pronunciation. Some words are spelt differently in the UK and the USA. A few publishers allow a writer to use either, but the usage must be consistent. Check whether a drug name that you are giving has different generic names in the USA and UK.

Stops or punctuation , ; : . NP

The common stops may still be considered to comprise a hierarchy: new paragraph, full stop (period or full point), colon, semicolon, dash, comma. The dash and the colon do not always fit into the hierarchy.

A new paragraph (NP), in general, denotes a change of subject. In good prose, one notion leads to another, which makes this rule difficult to apply. Because short paragraphs can look irritating, long ones boring, skilful compromise may be needed. If you want each new paragraph in your published paper to show, you MUST either indicate each one by indention or mark it on your script. [See p. xii.]

Colon. The phrase before a colon is general; the phrase (or phrases) after it is (are) particular. Therefore, no sentence should contain two colons. Traditionally a colon does not end a sentence, but a full stop does, so a colon should not occur after a phrase that refers to more than one sentence each having its own full stop. For example, if 'as follows' is followed by complete sentences, use a full stop, not a colon, after 'follows'. The following type of confusion is submitted to editors.

The solution contained: glucose: 2 g, NaCl: 3 g and urea: 4 g.
The piece is better written as follows.

The solution contained: glucose, 2 g; NaCl, 3 g; and urea, 4 g.
Similarly '. . . conditions (time: 25 min, current: 2 A)' should have its comma replaced by a semicolon and its colons by commas.

Some people would banish the colon; yet it can have a real use. Please help it to survive and to keep its value – greater than that of the comma, less than that of a full stop.

The semicolon differs from the colon in various ways: it signals a shorter pause; it separates items in a list; it joins closely related clauses.

The comma signals a short pause. Use commas cannily, and more often than some writers use them, to prevent over-reading – as in the next sentence. Where two adjacent nouns belong in different clauses separation should be achieved with a comma – for example after 'clauses'.

Children used to be taught not to put a comma before *and*. The logic is as follows. We may mean *a* and *b* and *c*, but we write *a*, *b* and *c*. One *and* is replaced by a comma, but no comma is needed before the retained *and*. In the phrases 'chalk and clay' and 'tides were measured and recorded' no comma is needed. The *and* is the joining variety and could be represented by &. There is another kind of *and*: 'the cats were fed on meat and worms were given to the fish'. Your probable hesitation could have been avoided if a comma had appeared after 'meat'. Here is another example: '. . . is dissolved in 5 mol NaOH l^{-1} and 2 mol KOH l^{-1} is added'. And another: 'The chairman was head of the physics lab and the principal of the maths lab was elected vice-chairman'. So, when two phrases are linked by *and* a comma is needed to show that they *are* two phrases. Curiously, the superstition does not ban the comma before *or*, or before *but*.

A comma is needed before an *and* that separates negative and positive notions, as in 'Do not write too much between full stops and present the information in small packets for easy understanding' and in 'The alloy is made by adding Sn to Pb and Zn is rigorously excluded'.

A comma can change or even reverse a meaning. 'The sky is not black, as Zob claimed' means Zob claimed the sky is not black. Without the comma the phrase means Zob claimed the sky is black. Consider these two sentences. (a) Scientists, who are honest, report what they observe. (b) Scientists who are honest report what they observe. Sentence (a) defines scientists as being honest. History shows that a few have been dishonest, so sentence (b) is preferred.

Commas are often used in pairs, *as here*, to enclose a parenthetical remark. The latter is treated at **1** (18).

A comma can change the meaning of a word. In 'However he added . . .', *However* means 'in what way'. In 'However, he added . . .', *However* means 'But'.

17) *Dashes.* The four symbols, hyphen (-), en rule (–), minus (−) and em rule (—), are represented on a typewriter and word processor by one sign popularly called a dash. Nowadays, a short dash (en rule) with a space each side – as here – usually replaces the long dash—the em rule—but the meaning remains the same. The meanings of the hyphen and the dash are opposite: the hyphen joins words or pieces of a word; the em rule pushes words apart with a pause longer than that signalled by a comma.

The hyphen and the dash are distressingly often confused even by educated people and trained typists. I appeal to you to persuade your colleagues to preserve the identities of these useful signs.

The en rule (short dash) has various uses, including that in 1978–89. Spaces are not needed. Write 'from 2 to 28' not 'from 2–28'. Solutions are sometimes described thus:

hydrochloric acid–sodium chloride

ethanol–ethanoic acid–water

Avoid confusion by writing 'mixture of hydrochloric acid and sodium chloride' or 'mixture of ethanol, ethanoic acid and water (3:1:10)'.

The hyphen has many uses. Because the rules cannot be condensed to a few lines I shall do no more than offer suggestions and examples.

A hyphen joins words to make adjectives: if a hypothesis is well known it is a well-known hypothesis; an example is the all-or-none hypothesis. Do not join adverbs that end in -ly. Write 'vitamin-deficient and rarely eaten food'; also write 'X-ray-induced and chemically induced mutations'. A hyphen can change a meaning: a large impulse counter is not the same as a large-impulse counter; 5 day sessions differs from 5-day sessions.

Hyphens may be used to join nouns to make an adjective (vanadium-steel pin, noun-adjective phrase), but if this be done with multiple nouns the result is clumsy, as in negative-particle-analysis procedure and Lipon-8B-column chromatography. Such phrases should be turned; e.g. 'ablacil-C-induced effect' should be 'effect induced by ablacil C'.

Consult a recently issued and well-produced catalogue for help with hyphens in chemical names. Catalogues from BDH [**8** (20)] have been useful.

Link a prefix (non-, post-, etc.) to a noun by a hyphen. T. W. Fline [p. xiv] are then warned to look in the dictionary for the noun instead of searching under n or p. Postparturition might confuse him. Insertion of a hyphen may aid the pronunciation of words such as sub-unit, co-operate and co-worker.

If you invent a new name, for example Q effect or HK thesons, do not use hyphens. 'Copper compound' should not be joined by a hyphen; nor should 't test'.

(18)   *Parentheses* is the name for round brackets ( ). Parenthesis also means an aside or explanation between two commas, dashes or parentheses (as here) within a sentence. If such a parenthetic remark is left out, the sentence should still make sense and be grammatically complete. If the remark is a complete sentence give it a capital letter and its own full stop, surround the whole with parentheses or square brackets, and place it after, not within, its parent sentence. [**4** (1).] Although '(Table 2)' may appear within a sentence, it is better for a longer phrase such as '(See for example Table 2.)' to be treated as a sentence. If the parenthesis is only part of a sentence, the full stop goes outside.

(19)   *The solidus* (diagonal, slash) is used to mean 'per' as in wires/cable. Confusion may arise if the diagonal is used for other meanings, such as dates or contractions. A solidus may make 'response/dose' better than dose–response.

A solidus brings a mathematical formula into one line, thus: $(a + b^2)/3p$. Fractions going through two lines are ugly.

The solidus should not be used for *plus*, *and*, *with* or meaning other than *per* except after careful thought.

Initial letters. Avoid starting a sentence with a lower-case abbreviation, such as p- or α-, or with *van der*, if you can. A sentence should not start with a numeral. If you find such a sentence, either rewrite it or spell out the number. This practice is especially important when the previous sentence ends with a numeral, symbol or abbreviation: change '. . . found in 1989. 73 µg of iodine was . . .' to '. . . found in 1989. Iodine (73 µg) was . . .'.

Abbrevns & cntrctns

The smallest symbol in the printer's fount, the dot (.), has many meanings. Its second best-known function is to indicate abbreviations. The abbreviative presence – or the absence – of the dot evokes more editorial adrenaline than does that of any of the larger symbols.
So here I indicate practices but do not dare to instruct.

Some publishers omit the dot from Expt, Mr and Dr as well as from other contractions that include the first and last letters of the word. Some words (Miss, log, bus) have been with us so long that few people give them a stop. Units (g, mm, F, min, h) take no full stop (period) and plurals no 's'. No dot is needed in acronyms: laser, radar.

A few abbreviations are ugly. *Viz.* saves only two characters from *namely*, and *c.* saves three from *about*. *Approx.*, too, is bettered by *about*. *Cf.*, which means *compare* not *see*, may usually be deleted.

The *Biochemical Journal*, in its instructions to authors [8 (2)], gives a list of abbreviations useful to all scientists.

Abbreviations of long terms, or of names of materials to which you often refer, are best collected on a page by themselves. The names should be given in full in the Summary.

Headings or captions

As a novelist uses dialogue to make a page look interesting, so a scientific writer uses headings and subheads. They help to make a paper readable, and guide inquirers to parts they want to read again. Use many. Write subheads for the Discussion; they can be truly helpful.

A heading should contain a noun. A lone adjective should not be used; add 'part' to Experimental.

Make your headings work. Be cunning. Perhaps you have used the 'in-other-words' device in the text but still desire emphasis. Try to include, in a heading, the notion that needs emphasis, but use different expressions in heading and text. [See **1** (15) on revision, or **4** (2).] Repetition of a heading in the text is undesirable. A heading may ask a question [**Ex** (1)]. The Introduction to a normal paper should not need that word as heading, which is as superfluous as is 'Notice' on an obvious notice. However, if you can put information into a heading for the Introduction, that could be useful. For example, can you describe your problem in words different from those in the Title?

Tables

Study the tables in the journal of your choice; then conform with the style so that the editor does not have to make rearrangements.

A table needs a title, probably supplemented by an explanation. The heading to each column usually includes units, so that each entry is a number. If your quantities are large or small, use the prefixes M, m, p, etc. Avoid using $\times 10^{-3}$ in a heading because a reader may wonder – have you divided by 10^3 or is it still to be done?

Indigestible tables with many or cumbersome values deter readers. Trim the values even if you risk losing an occasional significant digit. Methods exist for calculating significant digits. One digit more than is meaningful does no good whatever. Indeed, a writer who presents non-significant digits is displaying a lack of understanding. The s.e.m. should have no more digits after the decimal than does the mean. Should the argument require results from several experiments, and they cannot be condensed or pooled [see **1** (5)], consider dividing them into two or more tables.

When measures of variation are given there must be no doubt about their meaning. Common useful measures are the following.

The standard deviation (s.d.) gives an estimate of the spread of a measurable variable. The dimensions or units (pascals, mg/l, . . .) are those of the variable being measured.

The standard error of the mean (s.e.m.) gives an estimate of the precision of the mean.

The coefficient of variation (c.v.) is dimensionless and is useful in comparisons between populations. The c.v. is usually the s.d. expressed as a percentage of the mean.

Unfortunately s.d. and s.e. have sometimes been used interchangeably. In one paper submitted, the standard error of the mean was so described several times, but the formula, given three times (in text, table and note), was that for s.d. You may often encounter s.e. without the m. But common practice does not make it good practice. For clarity's sake include the m.

Illustrations

When an experiment provides many observations they may be better given in a graph than as a table. For many people a diagram is easier to grasp and to remember than is a table. The same information is not usually allowed to appear in both forms.

The horizontal co-ordinate of a graph represents what we select (time, weight, frequency . . .) and the vertical co-ordinate what we measure. If the origin of an axis is not zero, indicate this by a break in the line. A graph needs an indication of precision, such as an estimate of confidence limits, or symbols of a size to indicate the s.e.m.

Units & quantities

Use SI units. Some old units (e.g. bar, calorie, mmHg) may survive for a time, but, when old units are used, SI units should be given too.

Modern units go up and down in steps of 1000. Avoid other steps if you can. The ångström is redundant – and mispronounced! Concentrations other than mol l^{-1} are expressed as parts per thousand or per million (p.p.m.). Concentrations should no longer be expressed as %.

What is still sometimes called molecular weight is a ratio rather than a weight. This ratio is printed M_r. Dixon (1983) explains why relative molecular mass is a better term than molecular weight. The inferior $_r$ is typographically unsatisfactory, which may be one reason for the unpopularity of M_r. Another may be the resemblance to Mr (mister). See, for example, what looks like 'Mr. Dixon' above.

Make your units unambiguous. If you 'add 2 mol l^{-1} HCl', either say how much HCl you added or that you 'made the solution 2 mol l^{-1} with respect to HCl'. Better still, write 2 mol HCl l^{-1}.

Times should be given on the 24-h system, e.g. 08 h 30. Dates are printed without stops (06 April 1990) or with hyphens (06-iv-1990). Logically we should proceed from large to small units (year, month, day, hour, min . . ., thus 1990-04-06 . . .) as astronomers do and as we do with weights and measures. This logical system is described in British Standard 4795 [**8** (19)] and in ISO-2014; 1975.

When you offer a series of values, do not repeat the units. Write '3 and 4 g' not 3 g and 4 g. Another kind of repetition should also be avoided. From 'the percentage was 8%' omit % or write 'the proportion was 8%'. Write 'the pH was 8', and 'the voltage was 8' or state that the e.m.f. was 8 V. People do not write that the ohmage was 8 ohms or that the hourage was 14:00 h.

Units named after people are spelt without capitals but symbols for such units do have capitals: thus, watt and W, joule and J, pascal and Pa. Write lower case k for kilo.

Because l, 1 and I may be confused, especially in scripts and in sanserif (l, 1, I), L is better than l for litre. For an entertaining history of the origin of L, see Wolner (1975).

Good sense

Read other people's writings critically. Even edit them – but not in library books! Improvements can usually be visualized in, and words may be deleted from, MOST papers (as well as from Directives to Authors in some journals!) without effect on the meaning. You may obtain amusement by collecting oddities, and this will help you to be vigilant in avoiding them in your own writing. Here are some: absent in the solution (write *from*); molar $CuSO_4,5H_2O$; the kind gift; at (20) varying temperatures in a thermo*stat* (write *various*); our records show that you do not exist; pressure of space; specimens were stored in a refrigerator wrapped in Al foil; beam from a Philips machine filtered through 1 mm Cu; they were in fact not artifacts. The title of a paper seen in a medical journal: 'Prevention of recurrent sudden death.'

More desirable is the collecting of 'good stuff' [Herbert, **8** (11)]. When you meet good writing, study it. Try to analyse your liking for it. Then emulate it. Through attentive reading you can enlarge your vocabulary. This will help you to overcome a principal difficulty in writing: finding the right word. When you have this difficulty (quandary, problem, doubt, perplexity, dilemma . . .), write various words (as here). Later, you may choose (select, reject, pick, exclude . . .) suitably. If no word fits, consult *Roget's Thesaurus* [**8** (17)]. If you meet a 'new' word you like, look it up in a dictionary before you use it. Then you will be unlikely to write a howler such as 'two of the six quintiles'.

Emotion & modesty in scientific writing

May I suggest that you avoid emotion in scientific papers? 'Great importance', 'significant conclusions' and similar expressions should be restrained. If you are tempted to write 'this most interesting result' ask yourself 'To whom is it most interesting?' Strunk (**8** (10)) writes 'Instead of announcing that what you are about to tell is interesting, make it so'.

A system, e.g. blood clotting, may have several essential components. An experimenter says that the component he studied is important. What is he telling us? 'Important' is a superfluous term for an 'essential' component.

You must mention your publications as necessary, but do not let the Bibliography look like a personal history.

If Lob published first, write 'my result agrees with that of Lob' not 'Lob confirmed my result'.

An author who writes 'we were surprised' or 'unexpected result' admits lack of knowledge, for those who know all can predict all. Humility is good but may not be the author's intent.

(21) Promises should be offered only sparingly. Authors who write that an idea will be investigated may be warning you off 'their' territory.

Why omit 'other' from 'human and other animals'?

If you list arguments as 'first, . . . second(ly), . . .' avoid calling the last 'finally'. You can rarely be certain the subject is closed.

Of course we hope – but privately, not in a scientific paper.

The three saddest words in the language

'The Editor regrets . . .'. So what should you do?

First, do nothing, or at least nothing impulsive.

Second, take note of the reasons the Editor gives for non-acceptance and consider taking his or her advice. Most editors are kindly people.

Third, pay attention to what the referees say. [Reviewers in the USA.] They may have spent much time on their reports.

Fourth, read this chapter again. Read it slowly; you skimmed it too quickly last time.

Fifth, rewrite the paper. Then show it to two critical colleagues.

Chapter Two

Before you lecture or talk to us, please read this

Craftsmanship in speaking at meetings

Most scientists attend conferences and listen to talks by other scientists. Occasionally, a speaker so enthrals listeners that they enjoy hearing about the work and they listen intently. On the other hand, a speaker may be so dull, ill-prepared or inaudible that listeners fail to follow what is said.

Between such speakers are others, most of whom could deliver a better talk if they were helped. Some speakers may not realize that they could improve their performance. Many conference attenders have told me that they have suffered while striving to listen to such speakers. Because I have suffered too, I have been inspired to write this chapter. Books on lecturing exist, but scientists are too busy to read them. Perhaps they can find time to look at this chapter or at least to read about empty words and visual aids.

Direct style

Part of what I have written is in the imperative. This is because the imperative allows the most vigorous and most readable style. I write as though I am speaking to you because one day I may be listening to you.

Bad manners

If a scientist gives a talk without taking care to make it easily understandable, that is bad manners. Sometimes I think that a person other than the head of the Unit should be giving the talk.

The idea expressed in the first sentences in this chapter is so important that I shall repeat it but in a different form. Moreover, you may meet the idea yet again elsewhere. High you may be on the status

ladder, but, if we impatient listeners on lower rungs cannot understand
you, we shall not esteem you and your communication will be wasted.
On the other hand, if you enlighten us, your stature will increase.

Title of your talk

Look at lists of talks; some titles tell us what a talk will be about, some
do not. Ensure that yours does. Try it on colleagues. Avoid standing up
at the start of your talk to tell us that the title given in the programme
is inappropriate.

How to begin

Listeners may not hear the first sentence of a talk; they are 'tuning in'.
So do not start with crucial information. If you have to say 'it's an
honour to be invited . . .', let that be your opening, but limit it to one
sentence. If you do not need that opening, look to the back of the room
and ask 'Can you hear me?' I have done that; it works.

Now begin.

What to talk about

Please tell us

1, why you did this work;
2, how you did it;
3, what you found;
4, what you think it means.

Thank your audience (<6 words); then stop.

A scientific talk should not take the form of a written paper. You are
telling us of your recent discovery, so the first three parts make up the
necessary prelude to your main Message in part 4. In a written paper, a
scientist must so describe the method that another can repeat the
experiments. In a short talk, we must assume that your method was
suitable; a description of the principle of the method should suffice.
Anybody who wishes to pursue your experiments can speak to you
afterwards.

Part 3 should take most of your allotted time. You have to tell us
enough results to support your conclusion, but you must simplify them.
The results must not be cluttered with statistical details. Just tell us
the averages (for example from your experiments with and without

treatments) and their statistical significance; we have to trust that your calculations are correct. A graph is more easily understood than is any but the simplest table; the more results you have the more complicated is the table, but the better the graph.

Now tell us your Conclusion (part 4). This is what we have come to hear. So you must do all you can to convey this part clearly. Let there be no distraction: turn off the projector; do not rustle your notes.

Verbal delivery

Let us consider how you can make yourself heard and understood.

A good speaker looks at the audience, not at the furniture, but does not stare at any one person. Hold up your head and speak to people at the back of the room. Then those at the front should hear too.

Do not read your 'talk'. If you read, you may speak too fast or in a monotone; you will look down, compress your lungs and perhaps become inaudible. Speaking to your stomach will do it no good. If you *have* to read a passage, hold the book or paper high.

Notes as prompter

See p. 2, note 3 about 'reservoirs'. From such reservoirs, prepare notes; if they help, use them. There is nothing shameful about that. Notes are better written as headings than as sentences: then you can refer to them at a glance. Lettering should be large, clear and well spaced, in lower case, not capitals, so that you can read them without a lectern lamp. The lamp distracts listeners and casts unflattering light on your face. Make the note on cards the area of this page so that you can carry them if you walk to the wallboard.* When you think the notes are ready, go through them with a red crayon and ruthlessly slash out non-essentials. Number the cards. My (paper) notes were once blown to the floor by the projector's fan. How glad I was that they were numbered. Now I use cards.

On the top card, write a list or items to take into the lecture hall: clock, mask for the projector, coloured markers, pen, books, exhibits . . . .

If you have slides, apparatus, specimens, transparencies to exhibit, signal them with numbers on your notes – *in colour*. The audience will

---

* The blackboard is now often white or green.

not appreciate your: 'Oh yes; I should have shown this earlier'.
Numbers of the reminders should tally with numbers written on the
items.

Some speakers, not knowing what to do with their hands, put them
into their pockets. This is inelegant. Notes help, by occupying your
hands.

Stage fright

If you have delivered many talks or lectures, please skip this section.

If you are a novice, you may wonder how to overcome nervousness.
Most people are nervous before or during their first public talk. With
practice, the nervousness lessens. One man's knees shook violently as
he stood on the platform but he concealed the shake by holding the
table. Several talks later he felt only a trace of nervousness before, and
none during, his talks. People need practice, and the smaller their first
audience the better. This is just one of the reasons why every
laboratory or institute should have a tea club at which a researcher tells
colleagues what he or she is doing. If your institute does not have a
club, perhaps you can found one. [**1** (1).]

Starting with a large audience can be devastating, as the following
incident shows. The television broadcast had begun. The next speaker
was awaiting his turn. Suddenly he said 'Oh, my car!' and ran out. The
producer assumed the man had remembered parking his car badly. He
did not return . . . .

One precaution to take against stage fright is to observe continual
foresight against your notes going astray. You could [not many would]
make a copy to keep in a pocket. The knowledge that all is in order
helps you to relax.

If you let it be seen that you have not prepared your talk, and you
fail to speak coherently, the audience will not like you. However, if the
audience senses that you have taken trouble but have stage fright, they
will be sympathetic. A sensing of such sympathy encourages a speaker,
and the nervousness diminishes.

Verbal style

We, your listeners, prefer that you 'talk' to us rather than deliver a
formal speech. This calls for a simple style. Here are suggestions.

In general, use short sentences. But if they are all short, delivery will
be jerky. A pleasing sentence usually has two main verbs, but an

occasional very short sentence may be used for emphasis. (See the next paragraph.) If an interpreter is present, remember that simple sentences can be translated more easily than complex ones.

¶ Please finish every sentence.

Importance of deliberate speech

Speak so slowly that it seems almost absurd. There are good reasons. When we stand, heart throbbing, before an audience, adrenaline speeds us up, and we do not realize how fast we speak. During a lecture I was giving about speaking, I asked the audience to observe its pulse rate. The average was 65 beats per min; mine was 130. This was taken as evidence of my speed-up. When the experiment was repeated a dozen lectures later, my rate was only 75 beats per min. I had become adapted to lecturing and had to give a false value to make my point.

A maximal rate for speech is 100 words per min. So a 10-min talk should be kept to below 1000 words.

Rehearse your talk to a colleague, to a tape recorder, or to a video camera. Use a clock. Remember, the person who exceeds the allotted time is a thief and is also unwise, because a strict chairperson may call a halt before the Conclusion has been uttered. Ask your critic to time you and to tell you of your distracting mannerisms.

If you've not heard yourself before, you may be shocked when you hear the playback, as most of us were. Do you swallow the ends of words, as English-speaking people often do? Note whether you speak in an exPLOsive manner; this is disTURbing.

Utter no redundant words

If you are to speak slowly, yet have much to say, how can you resolve the dilemma? Contribute to a solution by uttering necessary words *only*; that is, aim at a high signal-to-noise ratio. Waste no words in saying you have not time to tell everything. Such non-information irritates the audience.

Omit: it has to be pointed out that; as a matter of fact; it only remains to be said that; the whole point is . . . . We have not travelled all this way to listen to such 'empty words'.

Avoid tautology [repeating, but with another word]: pooled together; foot pedal; circular disk; time clock; supplemented with additional salt; still remains; knots per hour. Obvious? Yes, but these double sayings do creep in. Whenever you see the offer of a 'free gift', renew your vow never to tautologize.

Andermanship makes us squirm in our seats

This striving for economy also means do not start sentences with 'Anderm', the most irritating non-word ever misfangled. When you listen to an interview on television, compare the interviewer's speech with that of the untrained interviewee. If you find yourself counting the times the latter says 'you know', 'that sort of thing' or 'basically' perhaps that will stimulate you to listen to yourself on a tape recorder, identify your personal in-fill word (or non-word), then train yourself to forgo it. That is difficult, but it can be done; it *must* be done if you are to become an Eloquent Scientist.

¶ I entreat you to read that last paragraph again. And then at least once more.

Speak deliberately; carefully choose good words. You can then offer more information per unit time than can those who talk fast and join phrases intoalmostinterminablesentencespaddedwith empty words and noise.

Hackneyed phrases

Clichés, such as 'tip of the iceberg', should be 'avoided like the plague', banished 'for ever and a day' 'and then some'. Can you recall a sillier phrase than 'corner of the globe'? The foreigner who thought redox meant red ox would be puzzled by 'quantum leap' used outside atomic physics.

Pronunciation

Think of T. W. Fline while you speak. [Page xiv.] Articulate each word distinctly for them, and pronounce even the unaccented syllables at ends of words. Then your own nationals will hear you too. (See also pp. 59–60 on speaking abroad.)

Technical words should be pronounced unmistakably. For example, pronounce the y in methyl and in benzyl as in 'by', even if it is not your local custom to do so.

People from Britain or from North America, when speaking in the other place, should remember that not only does pronunciation differ, but different words may be used. [Fume cupboard, hood; earth, ground . . . .] Therefore, misunderstanding must be forestalled.

If English is not your native language, read Chapter Five.

Key words

Your talk may depend upon our hearing a particular word. That word may be drowned by a local cough or scrape. Then we lose the thread. Therefore, write such KEY WORDS on the wallboard large enough for me to read them at the back. Point to each as needed. The shorter the word the more important this gesture. Do you see why? On your notes, write each key word IN COLOUR.

Partial deafness

Perhaps as many as one in four of your audience has a hearing defect and may not even realize it. The reduced hearing is not evenly spread across the auditory 'spectrum': usually the loss is more severe at high than at low frequencies, although there may be selective loss at mid frequencies. So an amplifier may not help. What *does* help is clear enunciation. That cannot be given in rapid speech; so here is good reason for you to

speak slowly.

Partially deaf persons understand best if they see a speaker's lips. So stand in the light and look at the audience. Be tidy, so that you are easy to look at.

Auditory impulses go from the cochlea to the brain. They are then converted into meaning. You can do experiments to show that the conversion takes time. The rate of this conversion or cognition becomes slower with age.

Words

Use short words where you can: start, not commence; try, not endeavour; often, not frequently . . . . An uncommon word may express a *writer's* meaning exactly. Examples occur in this book. A reader can consult a dictionary about an unfamiliar word. A listener cannot do that, so a *speaker* should avoid such words.

Vogue words, too, should be avoided, unless they are really suitable. Examples are: focus, restructured, breakthrough, situation. Some vogue words do not even have the meaning speakers ascribe to them.

Perspective, for example, does not – or at least *did* not – mean viewpoint; it means two-dimensional representation of three-dimensional objects. Before you say *perspective*, please consult a dictionary; then say *viewpoint* if that is what you mean.

Infinitely variable should not be uttered for *continuously variable* if one or both limits are finite.

Constantly is 'constantly' misused (as it is here) to mean no more than *often*. *Continually*, *repeatedly*, *regularly* or even *sometimes*, may better represent the desired meaning. Reserve *constant* for unchanging. Say constantly changing only if you mean just that. Only say invariably if you mean always; even better, say always. A speaker who says that bad weather constantly [or invariably] interfered with observations means annoyingly often, and he implies that the Law of Exasperation was at work.

Relatively and *comparatively* should be used only if things are to be compared. Alone, these words have limited meaning. So has 'a fraction of'.

While should be restricted to its temporal meaning; try *whereas*, *although* or even *and*. Similarly, *because* sometimes betters *since*. Did an author really mean '*A* began an experiment while *B* finished it'?

When you speak, use no foreign words for words that exist in English, even though you might use them in writing. [1 (14).]

Say (and write!) *less* material but *fewer* things.

Contemporary terms

Be up to date over units and technical terms. Young listeners who have to 'translate' archaic names may 'lose' your next sentence. Such terms as *condenser* (for capacitor) or *normal solutions* may not be familiar to those who have recently left school.

Wolf words

People needing a word having the sense of *very*, yet knowing that word to be dying, resort to *totally* or *extremely*. These words once had the sense of ultimate, utmost, the highest possible, but such words are losing that meaning: for example, 'utterly vital' has come to mean no more than 'necessary'. If a speaker exaggerates, listeners will find him out and be suspicious of his other statements. Aesop's tragic story of the boy who cried 'Wolf!' is still valid.

Do you think there is a difference between

completely empty and empty.
absolutely none and none, or
much more and more?

Can you truly say that anything other than perhaps the speed of light (electromagnetic radiation) is extremely fast?

Pronouns it & I

Speakers may say 'it' as a stand-in for a word so distant that we cannot recollect it. Be safe: repeat it. [Do you see the point? The *it* should have been *the word*.] Listeners cannot 'refer back' as readers can.

The word 'I' need not be avoided altogether. Try to convey your enthusiasm about your work to us. An occasional 'I' helps, although too many are bad. Of course, you will not call yourself 'we' – unless you are royalty, an editor, pregnant, or the spokesperson of a team. Sometimes a speaker says 'we' to mean 'you and I'.

Teleology

In a scientific talk on television the speaker may say 'the bird has developed a long tongue so that it can reach nectar', or 'bright colours have evolved in flowers to make them attract insects'. The speaker would be wiser to say 'because the insect . . . it can reach' or 'because the flower is coloured it attracts . . .'.

There seems to be no evidence that DNA can think teleologically; if it could, it would have provided scientists with the gift of eloquence.

Diversions

For various reasons, listeners find it hard to concentrate, and they are easily diverted. If there is an interruption beyond your control and people look away from you, tell us 'I'll say that again'. Your courage will be admired. Some diversions may even be induced by the speaker him- or herself. Therefore, eschew irritating mannerisms, magniloquent words and complex sentences.

Keep it up

Some speakers start well but gradually lower their voice. On your notes write an occasional reminder to speak up.

Courtesy requires attention to detail

You may think I am a critical fusspot and that these details do not interest ordinary people. But we are not ordinary people; we are special people. You would not be reading about speaking were you not a Special Person. Therefore I hope you will campaign with me for better scientific talks.

Questions from the audience

You may be asked about experimental details or about your Conclusion during the discussion. Anticipate critical questions, and be prepared to answer them succinctly; yes, succinctly because most of the audience may not be interested in one questioner's problem.

Visual aids

If you use a projector, let your tables be truly simple. Never display more results than the argument needs. Tables from published papers may not be suitable for the screen and may provoke resentment. So *make tables especially for the occasion*. Then project the most crowded in an empty lecture room. If you cannot read a display from the back of the room, remake the table. If an overloaded table is shown on the screen, or on the wallboard, listeners wonder whether to study the table or listen to the speaker. They may attempt both and in their confusion do neither, so the speaker might have achieved more without the display! Do not think that saying 'You need only look at the bit in the bottom right-hand corner' helps us to read an illegible slide.

If you make slides, read what Norris (1978) writes about their preparation. His essay is excellent.

If an indicator of magnification is needed, show a measured bar. On the screen, '×1000' becomes meaningless.

Before you use an episcope, or the epi part of an epidiascope, in public, check whether what it projects is satisfactory as seen from the back of the hall.

A hand-held illuminated arrow should be switched off when not needed. Some speakers wave it about distractingly, or even, unknowingly, set it down pointing at the audience. Switch off the projector immediately you have used it, even though you may need it again, and turn out the lights. The audience should pay attention to what you are saying now, not to what you displayed minutes ago; and they should not be dazzled by a bright empty screen. Write reminders on your notes.

Some speakers project notes on to the screen, then talk around them. This is undesirable on three counts: the room has to be darkened; the audience reads ahead; and the speaker tends to talk to the screen. These objections vanish if an overhead projector is used, together with a mask, although speakers must remember to address the audience not the projector.

Overhead projector

An overhead projector has advantages over a slide projector (diascope). (Appendix, p. 40.)

Before you prepare transparencies, take a white card and draw lines, about 20 mm apart, across it. If you lay a transparent film on the card, the lines will help you to arrange your words neatly. As a compositor says: it's the arrangement of the white spaces that's important. Prepare your transparencies with permanent ink, then use suitable dense water-soluble ink for numbering the transparencies, in accordance with your notes, as well as for marking during your talk. After the talk or lecture, your marks and the number may be washed off, but the original writing remains for re-use. Write with bold clear lettering, NOT IN CAPITALS. [4 (3).] Typewritten characters are too small. We are not entertained by the remark 'I suppose you can't see these numbers'.

Separate the slippery transparencies between sheets of white paper: (a) to lessen sliding; (b) so that you can read the top one.

Before you project, place a mask of card over the display; then move the mask to uncover what you want the audience to see as you speak. Do not first display the whole, *then* cover it; that is discourteous.

In a very large room an overhead projector may not be suitable. Another system must then be used.

Microphone & loudspeakers

Should you use a speech amplifier? If you have a strong voice and will speak up – no. Even the best systems give some distortion; and your freedom may be restricted. If you *have* to face the screen or wallboard, however, an amplifier may be advisable.

Light relief or humorous remarks

Should you tell a funny story? Yes, if it be relevant, brief, witty and dignified. Not otherwise. Favourable response from an audience dispels nervousness and helps you to speak better. And we shall listen alertly in the hope of more fun. Perhaps you can recall an incident from a previous lecture, or you may have seen an oddity such as 'Drugs were given to patients dissolved in alcohol.' Bear in mind that feeble or crude jokes will do no good and may damage a lecturer's image. Having no response from what the lecturer thinks is funny can be devastating.

Television & videotape

Speaking for television needs especial care because television loud-speakers are not usually hi fi. Before the talk, a speaker might ask the producer not to show a close-up in which the face fills the screen. If it does, viewers may study details of the face instead of listening.

This chapter does not tell everything

I have made suggestions. You can probably make others. There is space for them at the back of this book.

You may like to read Kenny (1983) on public speaking.

Formal lectures

My intention in writing this chapter (coming, as it were, from the body of the audience) was to appeal to those giving short talks. A graph of listeners' comprehension against time shows a fall within 10 min. So points about good speech and sensible delivery for short talks are relevant to 50-min lectures too. A joke at 10-min intervals stimulates us wondrously.

Directive for lulling an audience to sleep

Wear a dark suit and conventional tie; turn down the lights;
close the curtains (drapes); display a crowded slide and leave
it in place; stand still; *read* your paper without looking up;
read steadily with no marked changes in cadence; show no
pictures; use grandiloquent words and long sentences.

Appendix on projectors

We are told not to switch projectors off and
on needlessly because that harms the lamp. Switching need not be bad
if a thermistor has been fitted; every projector should have one. The
projector should carry a spare lamp, *in working order*.

Overhead projectors have several merits in comparison with slide
projectors, including the following. The room need not be darkened:
this facilitates note taking and the lectern needs no light. Projection is
under the speaker's control. The speaker can see the audience. A
display can be unmasked gradually. Displays can be developed during a
talk. Transparencies prepared beforehand can be written on during a
talk. Transparencies do not bulge and go out of focus. Insertion
upside-down is obviated. Transparencies can be prepared, or modified,
without photography and therefore immediately before a talk. Colours
are easily included. One transparency can be superimposed on another.
Big transparencies are easy for interested parties to examine after a
talk. If speakers prepare their own transparencies and write in large
lettering, they are less likely to put on too much than if someone else
makes the slides from typewritten copy.

Against this baker's dozen merits of overhead projectors there are
some demerits, but most of them could be overcome by better design
of the projector and of its immediate environment. Often the overhead
projector is placed on a table or trolley that is too low and the speaker
has to bend over, which is bad on several counts; also the speaker may
be dazzled when straightening up. If you are able to do so, ask to see
the projector before your talk and to have it raised. I have done that.
Sometimes I wonder, has that trolley's designer [a short person?] or the
head of the institute ever used the projector? A speaker needs more
than a narrow sloping lectern. A flat-topped bench is needed to provide
space for transparencies and other items. In some lecture rooms the
projector is sited out of reach of the speaker; much of the merit of the
projector is then lost. A quiet fan is desirable. A curved mirror might
be designed to lessen trapezoidal aberration.

If instruction on the siting and use of an overhead projector were
good, perhaps fewer people would resist using this admirable machine.
If you still think slides and a slide projector are better, list their
advantages. Can you produce even a dozen?

Chapter Ex
Empty numbers

Paradox

Scientists make observations to perhaps three or four digits, and process the results on an eight-digit calculator. Careful scientists then discard meaningless digits. They also use numbers and numerical words with care. But some writers use *words* with a precision corresponding to only one significant digit! Here are examples of these and other aberrations.

Doubtful ratios

The phrase '3 times more than' means '4 times as much as'. If this surprises you, extrapolate down to once more than, which obviously means twice as much as. Many readers take 'times more than' to mean the same as 'times as many as', so the former expression is best avoided. What does '4 times less than' mean? 'Once more than' means 'twice as much as', so 'once less than' must mean 'none'. Hence '4 times less than' seems to mean 'minus 3 times'.

'Every second baby is a boy' is not true. 'One in every two babies is a boy' is no better. By omitting 'every' we remove the absurdity. The words 'on average' might be added. 'Three in every 10 plants were diseased' implies a regularity that seem unlikely. A fine example [yes, it is genuine] that shows the absurdity is '$8\frac{1}{2}$ people out of every 10 . . .'. One's mind tries to visualize $\frac{1}{2}$ of a person instead of paying attention to the statistics. Better would be '17 out of 20' or 'more than 8 out of 10'.

'Decimate' originally meant kill every tenth man. Wise writers apply discretion in using the term for the elimination of more than a tenth.

Dilution

The term 1 : 4 is a ratio and is read as 'one to four'. For example, 'the ratio was 1 sheep to 4 goats' means 1 sheep in 5 goats, not 1 in 4. The meaning of 1 : 4 is different from that of 1/4, which has the sense of ¼. Some people read 1 : 4 as 1 in 4 and write 'diluted 1 : 4' when they really mean that the final volume was 4. The '1 : 4' is then wrong. Are you unconvinced? Then consider the term 1 : 1, which cannot mean 1 in 1. If you made 1 vol of solution up to 4 vols by adding diluent, then for clarity's sake write that. 'Diluted 1 in 4' or even '1 → 4' may be suitable for most purposes. If the exact dilution is important, you might write '1 vol solution A was diluted to 4 vols by adding solution B'. Bear in mind that 1 vol fluid A (e.g. ethanol or H_2SO_4) added to 1 vol fluid B (e.g. water) may not produce 2 vols of mixture.

(1) **Are all your numbers correct?**

If 'adviser' is misspelt, a subeditor can change that. If 27 appears for 21 a context may not help, so we are confused. Editors' time is wasted over wrong numbers actually detected, but the total of errors is unknown. In a table, nobody but the author can check the values. Draw a bar through each hand-written 7 to distinguish it from other characters.

Statistics

Standard deviation and standard error have often been confused. Yet they are the very quantities that are supposed to indicate precision! So take care that there can be no doubt and do not omit the M from S.E.M.

When n is small, these statistics have only little meaning. If an author offers statistics based on $n = 2$, the message conveyed to readers is that of desperation rather than useful discovery, and we may doubt the claims!

An often-seen phrase is 'most probably', which means highest possible likelihood, i.e. $P = 1$. Frequent use of 'most' debases its meaning.

Phrases to avoid

'Cages were built between 1988 and 1989.' Quick work indeed, for the interval is infinitely small.

'Twice the size' is sometimes written for twice the dimension. Because of possible misunderstanding, the former term should be used warily or not at all. If a picture's dimensions are doubled, its area is quadrupled.

A surface 3 m square has an area of 9 m². Some readers may not know that. Write 3 m × 3 m.

Do not write 3–400 if you mean 300–400.

'A plate 75 × 90 mm' is not scientific. Write 75 mm × 90 mm.

An experiment repeated 3 times is done 4 times. If you have doubts, consider 'repeated once'. 'Repeated again' might be considered tautological.

'Divided by a third' is best avoided. If the reader is not interested in decoding, the information is lost.

'A certain amount' usually means an uncertain or unspecified amount and is too vague for scientific reporting.

A speaker described a humming bird that lives in high mountains in Equador. He told us 'To conserve energy the bird's temperature falls to half at night'. What is half a temperature?

'Nearer 40 than 30' tells us only little: any number > 40 is nearer 40 than 30. We know what the speaker means, but should the language not have been more precise?

Percentages

The sign % indicates a pure fraction without units. The present tendency of using terms other than percentage for concentrations is admirable. A writer who describes a concentration as 5% and then writes 'it rose 2%' leaves you to guess whether 2 percentage units or × 1.02 is meant. Percentages are best reserved for comparisons. They must be clear. Replace '150% more than' by $2\frac{1}{2}$ times. What does '250% lower than' mean?

Do not write 'g/L of KCl' if the solution is not per litre of KCl but of KCl per litre. Equally unscientific, though common, is the note that 2 mg/kg of a drug were given. Write '2 mg of drug per kg' or 'drug (2 mg/kg)'. The argument also applies to 'p.p.m. CO_2'.

Do your readers demand too much?

Perhaps you think these comments are pedantic. Some may be. But scientific reports, written or spoken, should reflect the precision of the experiments. Numbers and values submitted to editors or presented at meetings are sometimes hardly better than 'umpteen zillion' or 'every so often'.

Chapter Four
Preparations of the script and figures

The script may be read by several people, usually by an editor, two referees (reviewers in the USA), a subeditor (copy-editor) or language corrector, the copy-preparer, the printer and the proof reader. This should be sufficient reason for the preparation of clear script. Yet poorly prepared scripts are commonly submitted to editors; I have seen some that were barely legible. Even a script that looks neat may not be good from the printer's point of view. This is partly because typists' typography may differ from that of printers as to spacing and punctu-

(1) ation. [Unfortunately the typist may have had to type in that manner to pass her exams.] After the subeditor and the copy-preparer have corrected and marked the typescript it may almost resemble a *manu-script*!

If you prepare the script yourself, please read this chapter carefully. If someone else prepares the script, please show them this chapter.

Spacing is important

The script should have wide margins, especially at the bottom. Standard left margins, say 40 mm wide, will help to ensure that pasted corrections are in alignment and that unintended indentations are avoided.

The script should be double-spaced throughout, *including that of footnotes, notes to tables and list of References*. That directive in italics is something often overlooked. It is not editorial pomp; the space is needed for instructions to the keyboard operator, and those instructions are usually more numerous in notes and legends than in the text. If you still desire to use close line spacing for parts of the script, make all spelling, punctuation, units, hyphens, capitals or lower case, decimals, formulas, numbers, etc. in accord with the style of the journal. If you cannot ensure all that, then leave interlinear space for the subeditor and copy-preparer.

44

The first line of each paragraph **should be indented**; three spaces are enough. A paragraph that is not indented (for reasons of fashion?) risks being 'run on', especially one that starts a page. This abominable non-indent fashion wastes the time of editors, who have to mark each new paragraph (NP) and who may have to turn back a page before they can decide whether an NP is desired. If you dislike indention in a script, or if the typing is done in a distant office outside your control, help the editorial staff by marking each NP with a □ on the final script.

Remember to change ug to μg and ul to μl. Many u's escape conversion. Ensure that symbols in legends, figures and text agree, for example 3*A* or 3*a*. Make fractions unmistakable; a reader took time to realize that 2.1/2 was not 1.05 but $2\frac{1}{2}$.

All pages must be numbered, *including the first page* as well as the list of References, etc. Imagine what happens if the script is dropped.

The journal may request two or more copies, and it should be axiomatic that good copies be submitted. Blurred script strains the referee's eyes because of the continual attempt – abortively – to sharpen the image by focusing. If you use a typewriter and its 'e' is full of fluff, clean it, for example with a toothbrush. Before you make photocopies, cut a tiny corner off each original page. Then you can identify the original and avoid making copies of copies. If your script is printed by a dot-matrix printer, remember to use the near letter quality mode. A script with fewer than 35 dots per character is unsuitable for scientific reports.

Typesetters appreciate good copy.

Directives from a Dutch uncle

Do you think these directives are stern? Experience shows that they need to be. I cannot recall having seen a script that needed no correction. Some scripts seem not to have been read, in final form, by the author. If a script has several authors, all of them should read it.

Bad script may not lead to a paper's rejection; but neither will it encourage the referee to read it promptly. Day [**8** (5)] writes that a badly typed script is immediately returned to the author. Another editor told me that poor script may delay publication by a month.

Word division at line ends

Do not split a word at the end of a line. If a hyphen appears there, the printer will usually join the parts of a word. If a hyphen is needed (as in dansyl-lysine), use a double hyphen (=) or repeat the hyphen at the start of the next line. Even better, take the whole word over, because broken wor- ds interfere with reading. The lines in a typescript need not all have the s- ame length. Do the unequal lines of this text disturb you as much as divided words would? When a scientific paper is to be typed, th- e machine should be instructed not to divide words.

Balloons (p. xii)

In the margin, write legibly or type 'Table .. near here' or 'Fig. .. near here'. Draw a ring or box round these and other directions to the printer about Greek symbols, mathematics, etc. Then the directions will not be printed. Such balloons are useful in other ways too.

Word processor (WP)

When a WP is used, some of the suggestions in this chapter do not apply. Corrections are so easily made on a WP that dirty pages should be corrected and printed afresh.

The WP has such advantages over the typewriter that the latter is seldom used for scientific script.

On the final copy of your processed script, you may have to add items manually: special symbols, complex underlinings, instructions, accents . . . . If the editor requires 3 copies, you need to make 5, including one to retain and one to deposit at home. To add all the items to all copies may be a laborious task and some items could be missed. Photocopies obviate the risk.

Does the VDU cause eyestrain?

Evidence for eyestrain caused by a fluorescent visual display unit (VDU) is scarce and conflicting.

If you think your VDU tires your eyes, consider the following.

Is your seating suitable?

Do you wear bifocal spectacles? The upper lens is designed for distant vision, the lower for close work (30 or 40 cm). Your VDU may be well over 40 cm distant, so neither of your lenses is ideal. Ask an optician about special spectacles or a pair with continuously variable lenses.

Cover sheet

(2)   Some publishers appreciate your supplying a top sheet. On it type the name of the journal, title of the paper, author(s), address for correspondence, running title, number of figures and number of tables.

Corrections and additions to the final copy

After a page has been retyped, check that all has been copied. If I cannot understand a passage in a typescript, I wonder whether a phrase has been omitted. Jumps occur when a typist 'picks up' a word in error at its repeat. (See 'tape . . . tape . . . tape' five sentences below.) When a WP is used, sometimes a line is lost or redundant material left in.

For small corrections, correct the text itself; do not make corrections in the margin as you would on proofs. Confirm by using a balloon if the mark is not distinct.

Corrections should not be attached with pins, clips or staples; they embarrass the printer. If you use transparent tape let it be invisible mending tape upon which one can write. Common self-adhesive tape should not be used. The latter, convenient though it is for authors and secretaries, is disliked by editors and typesetters, comes unstuck and cannot be written on. Flags, tails, flyleaves, turned-up pages and additions on the back of a page cause trouble, and their contents may even be accidentally overlooked by a referee or the typesetter. If more than a line is to be added, retype the page. Do not crowd the page. If there is too much for one page, type two pages. Then re-number the pages through to the end. Although the paper for all pages should be of uniform size, the lengths of scripts on pages need not be uniform. Short pages (script, not paper) are not troublesome, but long pages are.

Most of the directives in the paragraph above need not apply where a WP is used, but they need to be explained so long as some authors continue to provide typewritten scripts.

The typewriter's or word processor's type face

Before you buy a typewriter or WP, look for a type style that is suitable for scientific work. Sanserif (p. xvi) is unsuitable. If you have to accept sanserif and you show 'l' as part of a formula (e.g. ln, HI, -ol-1-one), name the symbol in the margin: ell, eye, ell, one. One day, while you wait in a queue (US 'line'), you may amuse yourself by recalling possible meanings of III; there are 4 or more. Where there is any doubt whether o, 0 or O is intended, whatever the type face, tell the printer what the symbol means: oh, zero, cap Oh.

Books on the preparation of printers' copy

Editors and others who prepare scripts for the printer will find useful information in *Copy-editing* by J. Butcher and in BS 5261. *The Oxford Dictionary for Writers & Editors* is especially useful to editors and subeditors. These books are described in Chapter Eight (13) onwards.

Numbering of figures, tables and references during their preparation

If you number the tables and figures from first writing you may have to change the numbers as your paper develops. Instead of numbers, use letters that describe tables and figures to you privately. Before the final typing, change to numbers. With this scheme you are unlikely to leave a wrong number in the text. On a WP, the letters or numbers are easily found if you follow each with @ or other sign that you otherwise never use.

Literature cited poses an analogous problem. At first I use the Harvard System: authors' names and year in the text. If the journal requires numbers, I change the script at a later stage.

Drawing the diagrams for reproduction

Draw diagrams about twice the *dimensions* of the desired printed version. Such enlargement demands thick lines, perhaps thicker than seem necessary to your eye. The lines of curves should be thicker than those of axes. Ensure that lines in different diagrams will appear equally thick, for example by using the same scale for all drawings. Insert the 'points' of a graph in ink. Sketch the curve first in pencil, free-hand or against a flexible rule. You can then erase the curve for re-drawing without losing the points. Or you may be able to calculate the line of best fit. The Biochemical Society's *Instructions* [8 (2)] give detailed directions on drawing graphs.

The printer likes drawings to be on smooth card, Bristol board or good tracing paper, but graph paper is usually acceptable provided its lines are faint blue. Graph paper helps one to keep drawings of apparatus square, so diagrams may be drawn on such paper. To transfer a diagram to Bristol board, fix the former on the latter, then prick through principal points with a needle. The tiny holes provide a template for your drawing. They will be inked over, and should cause no trouble.

Line drawings are reproduced by an all-or-none process. So draw your lines densely black; faint blue lines, pencillings, etc. are unlikely to appear on the printing plate. Deletions can be made with adhesive paper. You can make a continuous curve dotted or dashed by sticking narrow strips of paper over it at suitable intervals. Printed-pattern paper can be cut to shape and stuck over particular areas to make them hatched (shaded).

(3)
Write words or numerals on a transparent detachable overlay. Many printers can insert such lettering (labelling) onto diagrams professionally, but this possibility should be checked with the editor. An inexperienced draughtsman has difficulty in making the letters of suitable size. Examine a journal with author-drawn letters and you will see that unsuitable labelling spoils a picture. If you draw the letters or apply pressure-sensitive transfers, use lower-case letters; they are more legible than capitals. [See 'Legibility of print', **8** (1).] Label each curve if possible (seeking explanations in the legend is tiresome for the reader) but do not 'clutter' the diagram. The labelling must be brief, so as not to dominate the graphs. If there is not room for words on each curve, perhaps there are too many curves in the figure. Hers (1984) recommends the use of open ('empty') symbols for control curves; he also makes other good suggestions.

Draw a magnifier bar with scale value *on the picture*; then, if the picture is reduced, the bar is reduced too. A magnification number in the legend is unsatisfactory on several counts.

Journey's end for the script

If you write many papers or a book, visit a typesetter. You may then see what can be done and what is typographically costly. If you are shown examples of good and bad copy, you will see that the above homily on the preparation of a script is not too detailed. Further, you should see why alterations at the proof stage are expensive and may delay publication.

Chapter Five

Addressed to those for whom English is a foreign language

Errors of particular kinds occur in scripts and talks prepared by those whose first language is not English. The errors make the difference between foreign 'engelish' and idiomatic English. Errors of idiom distract a reader, and errors of pronunciation distract a listener. You want the reader to be attracted, not distracted. This chapter is intended to help you.

Words

Certain errors often occur in translation. Sometimes this is because an English word (control, eventual, sensible) resembles a foreign word that has another meaning. Other troublesome words are discussed below.

abolishment is not a word. Write abolition.

acknowledge. One may acknowledge receiving a gift, but one does not acknowledge a person for help; one thanks him.

adoption is probably not what you mean; try adaptation.

also commonly occurs in a wrong place; the best place is usually before the main verb. The same is true for **already**. The editor may delete the words because they are not always needed in the English translation.

both. 'Both wires were not hot' leaves it uncertain whether one of them was hot. Write 'neither wire was hot', if both were cold.

control, the verb, does not mean count, examine, inspect or observe, at least not in scientific English. Control means govern, maintain or limit a variable such as a rate of flow or a temperature. Measure, check or monitor may be what the writer means. Control, the noun, is well understood and needs no explanation.

could and **able** occur too often. 'We could measure' or 'were able to measure' tells only of the *ability* to measure. If you actually measured, say so: 'we measured' is definite. In 'the friction could be too great' perhaps the writer meant '. . . may have been'.

demonstrate is often written where another word would be better. The word has various meanings, the most usual being physically to display or show something happening. 'Nob reports that leaves of some trees contain gold' is more cautious than 'Nob has demonstrated . . .'. **Show** is less grandiloquent than demonstrate, but is not always suitable. Write 'the results show' [not demonstrate]; but write 'Cob has found' rather than 'Cob has shown' because he was writing about his experiments not showing them. 'Table 3 shows' is better than 'It can be seen in Table 3'. Usually, 'it has been demonstrated that' may be omitted: if you write about another's observation, write in the present tense; the meaning should then be understood and the five words are not needed. If you saw red grains among predominantly green grains, write that they were seen, not demonstrated.

describe is a transitive verb. You may describe a method or an apparatus. But 'Blob has described that chopped straw makes good fodder' is not good English. Write that he claims, states, writes or reports, or has claimed . . . .

dosis is not in common use; write *dose*.

eventually does not mean maybe. The event *will* happen – ultimately.

experience should not be written for *experiment*.

filtrated should be *filtered*.

insignificant, which means unimportant, should not be used in statistics. Write 'were not statistically significant' and quote the P value, or write *non-significant*. If you have no P value, you may write *negligible*.

know should not be used in the sense of to provide knowledge. 'The fossils were studied to know . . .' is not good. Write 'we studied the fossils to find out . . .'.

obtain means acquire, be given. Manipulations *provide* (not obtain) material. *Obtain* has the sense of acquire or fetch rather than of give.

quantitate is not (yet) a word in English dictionaries. You may quantify the effects though that is a grandiloquent word for measure or count.

registrated is not a word. A variable may be registered on an instrument such as an altimeter; readings from it are usually *recorded* rather than registered.

resorption should not be written for *absorption*, except in re-absorption, or for the special case of resorption of a foetus (fetus), limb or other part originally produced by the body.

respectively. In 'we cleaned the sherds and tiles, respectively' the word respectively is not needed, but is needed in 'we cleaned the sherds and tiles with water and oil, respectively'. Change 'blue respectively red' to 'blue and red, respectively', and do not shorten to resp.

since. Write 'seven years ago' not 'since seven years'.

supposed may be bettered by 'believed', for example, in 'birds are believed to have evolved from dinosaurs'.

Idiomatic English

Some common errors of idiom will now be discussed.

'Powder was added and stirred' is not good sense. Write 'Powder was added and the mixture was stirred'.

The abbreviation a.o. is not in common use, but 'etc.' is. The abbreviation for number is no. not nr. [**1** (13).] The term *aqua dest.* is best avoided.

'This permits to do that' needs an operator after permits; e.g. us.

Patient, the noun, is a sick person; *patient*, the adjective, means having *patience*. So patient blood means blood having patience! Write 'blood from patients' or 'patients' blood'.

Things compared must be comparable. 'Growth was similar to the controls' needs 'that in' before 'the'. 'Resonances in pipes were unlike rods' needs 'those in' before 'rods'. 'Lymphocytes from treated patients were larger than untreated patients' needs 'those from' after 'than'.

Spelling and pronunciation

Certain words are commonly misspelt: occurred, subtract, oxidation, centrifuged, homogeneous, synthesize, desiccate, naphthol, phthalic, saccharide. If the pronunciation of a word is changed, the meaning may also change. *Lead*, the noun, pronounced ledd, means Pb; the verb, pronounced leed, means to conduct. *Live*, pronounced liv, is a verb that means to be alive; pronounced lyve, it is an adjective describing an organism that is alive. Never pronounce the word as *leave*, which means go away. 'Live [lyve] fishes may be seen in the river where they live [liv]'. [Do you think English is illogical? Yes, it is.]

Use of a dictionary to check meanings of English words

In your Spandanese–Engels dictionary, you may find a word you want in English. Next, back-check the English word in your Engels–

Spandanese dictionary. Then consult an English dictionary (Chapter Eight) to confirm that the word is what you want. This procedure will help you to avoid writing *spatial cubicle* when you mean *spacious cubicle*, *vaulted caterpillar* when you mean *arched caterpillar*, *favourite* for *favourable*, *sensible* for *sensitive*, the colour is exactly different, or that the animals' diet was spiked with vitamins. You might be embarrassed were you to see, in print, that you had written permissiveness for permittivity.

While you are using the English dictionary to check the word, note how it is pronounced.

Speaking at conferences

Unless you have often conversed in English, try to find someone who will check your pronunciation. If you em**pha'**size in**corr'**ect syl**la'**bles the audience has to interpret words and may lose a sentence during the time it takes you to do that. A lost sentence may jeopardize your argument. So just one mispronunciation may ruin your talk. Forestall such a tragedy by displaying important words in writing.

I tried to follow a talk where the key word was spoken many times, always mispronounced, but never written down. For me, at least, the message failed.

International conventions

Use the international decimal point (0.6 g) for papers in English unless your publisher prefers the comma (0,6 g). Write 100 000 not 100.000 or 100,000 if you mean one hundred thousand.

Encouragement

For your comfort I may add that English people, too, find it difficult to write good English.

When you visit England or any other English-speaking country, or when you watch and listen to television from such a country, you may be appalled by the poor quality of parts of the speech you hear. You probably have a better knowledge of grammar than do the inhabitants. You may even be able to help to maintain the quality of what is now the International Language, especially when you become an editor. I hope you will do that; I have known Continental European scientists who have done so and I have learned from them.

Chapter Six
An appeal to North Americans

There are more of you than there are of us British. So you are now the Trustees of English, the International Language. Sad to say, not all of you are taking your trusteeship as seriously as you might.

One language

English, *at its best*, is much the same on both sides of the Atlantic. We spell some words differently, but we mostly understand one another. Some words are spelt more phonetically in the USA than in Britain. One day perhaps we shall have a unified spelling. Several words for food, transport and domestic items are different; but in science the differences are few.

Please understand, I do not suggest that, where American English and British English differ, the British version is always the better. The form more easily understandable by T. W. Fline is the better. T. W. Fline are **T**hose **W**hose **F**irst **L**anguage **I**s **N**ot **E**nglish. Imagine them to be looking over your shoulder as you write.

Grammar

British and American writers may be equally remiss in their treatment of English grammar, so I refer you to the section in Chapter One (p. 8).

Complex clumsy long-winded adjectival phrases

What Woodford (**8** (3)) calls stacked modifiers are prolix and at times barely comprehensible noun-adjective and modifier groups, as are this one and the heading above.

Consider 'voluntary human kidney donor research institution personnel'. A reader sees 6 words before realizing that the writer means people not kidneys. The reader of 'barley root tip cell chromosome aberrations' sees 5 false nouns before finding the real noun. The five checks or hold-ups tire the brain. The phrase would be better as 'chromosomal aberrations in root-tip cells of barley'.

The US journal *Science* carried correspondence on 'adjective noun use tendency'. Hildebrand (1983) gave examples of shockingly cumbersome phrases, and suggested that 'of' should be used to improve them. On the other hand, Baer (1983) disliked 'measurement of the angle of the joint of the ankle' and thought 'ankle-joint angle measurement' was better. Better still would have been 'measurement of the ankle-joint angle'.

So far as practicable, stacked modifiers should be avoided in writing and in speech. [See **1** (7).]

Future tense

Students in non-English-speaking countries learn that *shall* and *will* are used formally for the future tense but that *to be going to* is usual in speech. Which do you prefer: 'he's going to repeat' or he will repeat?

Americanizations

An Americanism that makes editors wince is the making of long words by adding -ize, -ism or -ization. Examples are prioritized, de-logarithmization and summarization. If you see such words, perhaps they will remind you to persuade colleagues and your research students to abstain from such 'manufacturization'.

Short words are often preferable to long words

T. W. Fline should not be conditioned, by example, to use ponderous words where simple words are adequate. Here are examples: methodology rarely betters method; enzymatic is less elegant than enzymic; detoxification is no improvement on detoxication; are experimental animals killed, or sacrificed? *Subsequently to* is a grandiloquent synonym for *after*. *Following* is no better, as this example shows: 'A still-thirsty cat was seen following a drink.'

In most US journals, the 'al' has been dropped from physiological, symmetrical, serological and other words. If these shorter words are acceptable, can you drop other needless syllables too? for example from sonification.

Export

You may point out that complex modifiers and ill use of words occur in European and other writings. True, but (*a*) not so often as in the USA, (*b*) they may have originated in the USA, and (*c*) that is no defense for their perpetuation in US journals or books that will be sold abroad. Please read again the first words of this chapter.

When Americans export words they should be careful to ensure that what they export is good. The export may be unwitting, but it occurs none the less, through journals, conferences, television . . . . People abroad copy what Americans write and say – the bad as well as the good. 'Prior to', for example, is becoming common in foreign writing; 'effect' and 'affect' are wrongly interchanged, as are *alternate* and *alternative*.

Please take care over these and other words, including such vogue words as basically (usually best omitted), dimension, situation, exotic, framework and secret.

In chromatography, a column of adsorbent, sometimes called the bed, is held in a tube. The tube is the support; it is not the column. In the USA, the word *column* is often used for either. This confusion has been exported; so, when a writer in any country states the length of a column, the reader cannot always tell whether the length is that of the container or the contents; the latter is what matters.

Corn, a general term abroad, means grain or cereal. In the Americas, corn usually means Indian corn or maize; in wheat-growing countries, corn may mean wheat. So, when a scientist speaks or writes about maize, or maize oil used in diets, he or she should give its Latin name (*Zea mays*) at the first mention, because some of the listeners or readers may be foreign. Likewise, 'corn oil' should be defined.

Homonyms, words with more than one meaning

Homonyms are a fact of everyday life; but in scientific writing, where communication must be precise, certain homonyms can introduce ambiguity. This problem is multipled in some transatlantic transfers. For example, formerly, to fix meant to make secure; in the USA, 'fix' is used for dozens of meanings including mend, destroy, mix, arrange and repair. This plethora of meanings confuses foreigners whose lexicon tells them that fix means fasten. Does 'he fixed the blockage in the apparatus' mean that he made it permanent or that he cleared, i.e. *un*fixed, it? In mutation research, 'genetic lesions were fixed' has the *opposite* meaning of genetic lesions were repaired. When 'repair' is eventually lost, perhaps the word will persist only as jargon in molecular biology!

Most of the words in the USA that have so far taken over the meanings of other words are used generally rather than for science. However, unless the Trustees are vigilant, this 'homonymization' will continue to invade scientific communication too, as the following examples show.

Localized is sometimes used for *located*. The latter means that something is situated, or was found, there; the former means it is only there.

Thus is often used where *hence*, *so*, *therefore* or *evidently* might be better. The original meaning of *thus* was *in that way*. Should we not keep it thus?

Manuscript means something handwritten. Neither a typescript nor the product of a word processor is a *manu*script. So let us leave the word to describe manuscripts, and use 'script' for a mechanical product. Thus (= in that way) we can make a distinction and often save 4 letters.

For *transportation*, i.e. the act of transporting, *transport* (train, cart, bus etc.) is used for the purpose. In the USA the longer word is used for both meanings. On occasion, the two meanings might be needed unequivocally in the same passage.

Practical and *practicable* are sometimes interchanged. The wearing of goggles in a laboratory is practicable in the sense that one is able to wear them, but vizors are more practical because they are ventilated.

A *referee* reads a paper and makes recommendations to the editor. A *reviewer* writes reviews for publication. There are two words for two meanings. In the USA, *reviewer* is used for both meanings.

Diet formerly meant the food of an animal, including humans. Now *diet* has become common usage for restricted food for certain people. Sometimes we need the early meaning, for example in studies on energy values. [See next paragraph.] We need another word.

Animals are given a diet, not fed the diet. One may feed an animal, but one cannot feed a diet. A US author 'fed a piscivorous diet'. He probably meant that his animals, not his diets, were fish eaters.

If *bred* is written for *mated*, readers outside the USA may not understand. Mated is understood internationally to mean that a male and a female were brought together for reproduction. Bred has another meaning: after many selections and matings [or cross-pollinations] a new strain of animal [or plant] may be 'bred'.

In Europe, *stones* and *rocks* have different meanings. By using *rocks* for both, you may be losing a useful distinction. If you say *rocks*, a European might not know that you mean *stones*, rocks being thought of as bigger than stones and usually fixed to the world.

Ensure and *insure* have two meanings, two spellings and two pronunciations. Only 'ensure' (to make sure) is likely to be needed in scientific communication, but do you not think we should keep the separate spellings?

Practice (noun) and *practise* (verb) are two words abroad. Has something perhaps been lost by the confusion of the spellings in the USA? A similar question might be asked about licence and license or tyre and tire.

The adjective *alter'nate* refers to a happening to one thing *then* the other; *alter'native* implies a choice of one *or* the other. To **al'**ternate is the verb. Electric current that alternates is called AC; DC is an alternative to AC. In an AC circuit, each pole is alternately positive then negative and so on.

Substantive is not a good alternative for *substantial*, because nowadays the former is used in specific legal and political phrases.

To *quit* means to go away from, to leave. In the USA the word is used to mean *cease*. In scientific writing it would be better to use stop, desist, refrain . . . .

With words being 'sacrificed' or made to double up, T. W. Fline hope their Spandanese–Engels lexicon will not become out of date faster than the publisher can cope with change. In a US dictionary, you may find some of these alternative meanings of given words. Dictionaries do not instruct, but report usage. For T. W. Fline's sake, please do not provide them with more material for 'homonymization'.

Careful choice of words

An essential of good English is that each phrase shall have only one meaning. That cannot be achieved if words 'stand in' for others. A scientist who wants to be understood abroad should remember that clarity is more important than whimsical fashion.

Hopefully is often used ambiguously. Were I to write 'Hopefully you will agree with some statements' that would mean you (not I) hope. So it would be truer to write 'I hope you . . .'.

Due to and *owing to* have different meanings, as explained at **1** (12).

Maybe it is too late to save pistol, stones, mend, locate, owing to, candy and other words with particular meanings. However, if the decay continues, your grandchildren may not be able to read and understand Mark Twain's books. Does that sadden you?

Of course you cannot be expected to give up established idioms, such as 'this moment in time', face 'up to' a problem, meet 'up with' a colleague, institutionalized, flat, make (for arrive at). Nevertheless, examples are given in this chapter to remind you of the trend and to reinforce the Appeal to you not to let *other* confusing usages or lengthy phrases become established. A professor in Minnesota said you cannot *reverse* the flow of the Mississippi; however, in view of your other engineering feats, I believe you could *control* the flow.

Speaking abroad

Naturally, you may not want to see the demise of local speech, be it Southern USA, Scots, Cockney or other. Each of us may think his or her way of speaking is correct and that the world should concur. The world does not concur: pronunciation depends on usage. Words are spoken differently in the Americas, Europe and elsewhere, so care must be taken over pronunciation whenever some listeners may be from outside a speaker's region.

The southern English pronunciation of path as parth seems odd to Americans. Likewise the American softening of 't' that produces twenny, madder and wahder puzzles foreigners. Metal mercury and methyl mercury are poisons that act differently. In a television program a speaker pronounced metal as meddel and methyl as methel (soft 'th' as in weather). At least one listener outside the USA could not distinguish the two words, so the gist was lost. In a lecture, a foreigner was baffled because 'isolated' was pronounced issolated. A Californian professor pronounced carotene as keratin. This caused a distraction until listeners became used to it.

Whether you say ameeno acid or amyno acid is unimportant. Whether you say vytamin or vittermin, we shall understand you. However, the formerly mysterious 'accessory food substances' were known to be vital and were at one time believed to be amines. So 'vital amines' became vitamins and were pronounced vytamins.

When you take part in an international congress or in a television program, speak slowly. If you have so much to tell that you must race, you will not achieve your objective if listeners cannot understand you. To gain time, use short words ('use' (noun) not 'utilization') and utter no needless words (very, really, invariably, up to). If we cannot understand you, we shall not respect you; but if we enjoy hearing (or reading) what you tell, we shall revere you.

One way to help listeners is to speak according to CBS English. I would find that difficult, so I understand that others might too. At least it should be tried for technical terms, which need especial care.

A good way to help yourself to speak well is to write a book on lecturing. Please write it for an international readership.

Papers submitted to foreign journals

Many US writers send papers to European journals. One editor said the best papers are excellent but the worst are not as good as those from writers whose first language is not English; he thought the spread of quality was too wide. My editor at CUP, evidently knowing this, asked me to write the present Appeal.

Caring Americans ARE concerned about the trend

In case you think that I am biased, let me remind you that authors of American books on writing also dislike the bad features discussed here.

Houp & Pearsall, in their excellent book [**8** (4)], give a list of pomposities to be avoided. If you have not read their Chapter 8, you have missed (out on) a treat.

Day [**8** (5)] instructs scientists – firmly – to use short words.

Woodford's (**8** (3)) piece on stacked modifiers, mentioned above, deserves study. He wrote it in the USA.

Nicholson's *American–English Usage* [**8** (9)], though out of print, deserves to be in print. She argues eloquently against careless writing; her own prose provides pleasant reading.

Holman (1962) writes 'Inelegant writing may charm the writer, but . . . offends the reader'. He quotes several abominations, including 'We horizontalized the patient . . . and decholecystectomized him'.

An American scientist (David E. Green, later to become a professor at the University of Wisconsin) instructed me, a research student, in scientific writing. He taught me, among other things, only to write an 'it' that would easily be related to a noun. He was careful to say 'I have to' not 'I gotta'. I learned much from him.

Editors of several US journals are evidently particular about English. Articles in *Scientific American*, for example, as well as papers in various other journals, are (mostly) noticeably well written and edited.

Editorials in *The New Yorker* are written superbly. *The New England Monthly* has established the Grammar Police to bring errors to the attention of offenders.

The annual Gobbledegook Award is an American institution.

Obviously, then, some Americans do care, and care very much, about the future of the language of science. Alas, they are not a majority. If more US scientists wrote as one of you (Strunk, **8**(10)) recommends, this chapter might be unnecessary.

How large is your vocabulary?

An ample vocabulary is a necessity for every scientist, although the interpretation of ample is arguable.

Will you do an experiment? Open a dictionary; on one page, count the words whose meanings you know; turn to other pages, then count . . . ; divide your total by the number of pages you examined; multiply this average by the number of pages in the book. Then compare your grand total with the three-quarter million or more words in English. I have done that; the result was humbling. If your score is a single-digit percentage, consider keeping a dictionary near the dining table. When the family argues about a word, consult the dictionary. That will increase the family's word power.

Useful American words

Sad to say, Britons have dropped some early words that you have kept (gotten, fall, closet . . .). The US use of *presently* to mean *at present* betters the UK use to mean *soon*. *Faucet* is hardly known in Europe, although it betters *tap* because the latter has various meanings.

Nevertheless, the world does know many of your words. *OK* and *radio* are universal. *Hindsight, dangling participle* (such as 'offspring were born 6 weeks after *mating*') and *blurb* are in common use. *Opine* (though many hate it and only few say it) is more apt than *figure*, which does not mean believe. The world knows that a wrench is the same as a spanner, even though the former hints at cruelty to nuts.

American wordsmiths have invented these words. So why do they not invent others when they are needed instead of using existing words for new meanings? Alternatively, since Britons accept so many of your words, why not accept some British words? Or consult *Roget's Thesaurus*? [**8** (17).]

Words that give no useful information are not needed and could be left out

Scientists of all nationalities write and say what Houp & Pearsall [8 (4)] call empty words. The use of certain of these words was, until recently, peculiar to North America. '*Right*' is an example; in what way does '*right here*' differ from *here*? The superfluous '*right*' and other words (*up with*, *out on* . . .) are *right now* invading '*up*' Europe and are being uttered in scientific talks. The Trustees should set a good example by leaving them out, unless a special shade of meaning is desired.

Because Americans invent such pithy phrases as 'Tuesday through Friday' and because $t = \$$, is it not odd that they write 'in the neighborhood of' or 'along the lines of' for 'about', and 'in the event of' for 'if'?

Data

Data once meant things given (or known) that could be used in argument. Readings from an instrument were not yet data. The raw results had to be averaged and perhaps processed in other ways. The data so derived could then be used to support or refute a hypothesis. Not only is it too late to reclaim the early meaning, but a further change looms, namely singularization. [What a word!] Data was plural. Many people would keep it so. If you agree, you may also think that 'the data presented' or 'the given data' is tautological.

Data is pronounced variously [dayta, dahta, datta, dadder], so speak the word clearly. A speaker may say 'Right now we're gunna subject the data to computerization'. During the time it takes us, the bemused foreigners, to interpret the phrase to mean 'We shall now analyze the results', the speaker may utter another sentence which we shall miss.

Evolution of language

Languages evolve; English is a blend of at least three. Slang becomes respectable. We cannot fix English for ever. But, instead of letting it slide aimlessly, we (all of us) should pay attention to the manner in which we let English change.

A professor of linguistics explained that the USA, a 'young' country, innovates fast and that Americans use an existing word in a novel way 'for the sake of change'. On the other hand, it seems sensible that useful words should be kept alive, including shall, will, results, maize, alternative, locate. Irregular verbs and irregular plurals could be made regular. [Agendas and medias are already on the way in.] A new word might be made for one of the meanings of a word that now has two, e.g. plasma.

T. W. Fline would welcome such changes, and others too. They might add 'Why may we not write "two times", sheeps or depend from?'

Too much rigidity would stultify the language, but, if we must alter it, let us be sensible in doing so.

Our obligations to T. W. Fline

If you think I am unkindly critical, please bear in mind that many people hold similar views and that several of the examples have been provided by editors. We, Americans, British and others, are fortunate in having the International Language as our mother tongue. Let us help T. W. Fline by restraining abusage and improving good usage.

Chapter Seven

Preparation of a doctoral dissertation or thesis

A thesis is like an unusually long paper, includes a review and is usually divided into chapters, so it resembles a book. Much of the detail that is described in other chapters of this monograph applies to the writing of a thesis. Although the style should be *concise*, no part should be so *brief* as to risk being inadequate. [The words concise and brief have different meanings but are often confused.]

Specialization

If you have worked mainly on your own, rather than in collaboration with a supervisor, you may have come to know more than anyone else in the world about one narrow subject. So you must explain your problem fully.

Collaboration

Most research is done by teams. If you worked with others, you must do your utmost to make it clear what parts of the work reported were yours. The examiners (assessors) will be especially curious to know how much you contributed to the thinking, the initiation and the conclusions of joint work. Write about this in a Preface.

Your own work

At the oral examination, the examiners, in asking questions about your interpretations, may be trying to find out whether your thesis was genuinely your own work. At one extreme the supervisor or advisor (US) almost writes the thesis. The other extreme was shown by the attitude of my supervisor: when I asked whether he would comment on the thesis I had written for a fellowship, he declined on principle and was somewhat shocked at my asking. If you write the thesis entirely yourself, use the same words as you would in deliberate speech; grandiloquent words will do no good. If English is not your native language, and someone helps you with language correction, obtain their permission to give their name in the Acknowledgements.

Imaginative evaluation of previous reports

In a thesis, the literature may be more fully reported than in a paper. Even a history of your problem may be acceptable if you can make it interesting. Discuss published work critically but not unkindly. Examiners like to know that you can evaluate other people's reports.

Looking ahead

Your inconclusive experiments may be mentioned and used as a basis for suggestions about what might be done next. Indeed, unlike a scientific paper, a thesis is a suitable place in which to propose experiments to test a hypothesis. [But see Promises, 1 (21).] Intelligent speculations, too, may have a place in a thesis. The examiners may even ask you about future hopes and intentions.

Allow enough time for careful correction

If you heed the advice given on p. 2 (When to begin writing), you must start your thesis before you are two-thirds through your course. You may think this is absurd because you have so few results. Even so, you can start on certain parts, as suggested on p. 3. The examiners may be seeking answers to the questions 'Does this student know how to set about a problem? Can he (or she) think?' rather than 'Has he (or she) done many experiments?'.

Physical presentation of the script

When you set out a thesis, consider the reader. Do not merely copy the style of another thesis or offer a cluster of assorted reprints and photocopies.

Examine well-designed books and arrange your thesis as a printer would. Write many headings or sub-heads [some people call them captions] and make a clear distinction between different kinds. Copious headings in the Discussion are especially important. Pages of script without sub-heads look stodgy.

If you have already published papers on subjects related to one another, combine them into one narrative, then type the whole. ['Type' includes composing on a WP.] Type the combination yourself even if you later give it to a professional typist for final preparation. As you type, you will edit and improve the script more effectively than if you only read it. If the thesis has many non-standard signs, symbols or pictograms, it may be well to consider producing the whole thesis uniformly by calligraphy. First find out whether that is allowable. The calligraphy must be clear and simple without swash letters.

Attend to the recommendations in Chapter Four. Examiners who find sloppy presentation may suspect that the experiments were sloppy too. Leave ample margins, with that at the foot greater than that at the top. A scanty bottom margin makes the script seem to be sliding off the paper. If the paper is A4 or near that size and the sheets are stab bound (stapled through the margin), the script should be no wider than 140 mm; a wide left margin is essential. [This may not apply in countries where the thesis is printed as a book.] If the bound volume will be too thick for stab binding, perhaps you should make two volumes. If, for this or any other reason, your thesis is in two volumes, make it clear that this is so, both on the covers and on the title pages. The two assessors of one Ph.D. student each examined a different volume without realizing there was another.

Give a complete table of Contents (but do not call it an index) and another of figures. Of course, if you *can* supply an Index, that would be impressive, but there is rarely time.

Explain the abbreviations you have used and arrange them as a list on a separate page or pages.

Place the Summary before the Introduction.

Several small tables are better than a few large ones. Place them, and the diagrams, near the relevant text; the smaller the table the easier this becomes. Arrange tables, diagrams and pictures upright (portrait fashion); readers dislike having to turn books sideways to study 'landscapes'.

Think about response/dose curves and related subjects in logarithmic terms. If one adds 1, 2, 3, 4, 5, 6 units of reagent, the jump from 1 to 2 is 1 unit but the concentration is increased $\times 2$. The jump from 5 to 6 is also 1 unit but the relative increase is only $\times 1.2$. For some studies it is better to arrange that each rise is proportionally the same. If your graph is then crowded at one end, try a non-linear scale. Convert doses into log doses or use log graph paper; or try reciprocals, squares or square roots; try dissimilar conversions for the two co-ordinates. Such

(1)   conversion may use the graphic area more effectively, and it may *reveal* a straight line.

The Conclusion

Your Conclusion, if you have one, warrants a section or even a chapter to itself. If it is only a few lines long, leave it so; do not pad it out.

Raw results must be processed or digested, by you, to provide data for use in your argument; but numerical values should not be prominent in the Conclusion. The latter should, in general, be in words supplemented by a minimum of numerical values if the subject allows that.

You should correct the script yourself

Every research student should read Clark (1960) on preparing for research, if the book can be found. The prose is a joy to read.

Various books have been published on thesis writing. A good essay is that by Hawkins (1982). He warns that an assessor may check some of the references for accuracy. He writes about 'errors that have occurred'. The errors include: misquotations; tables upside-down; bad captions; masses of complicated data with no explanation; statistics that make no sense; incorrect references; words left out; and literal errors. The use of the colloquial 'horrendous' seems appropriate here. So be painstaking over the preparation, reporting of results, spelling and punctuation; there will be neither editor nor printer to put those in order for you. The thesis will be with you for life.

One often finds the standard error of the mean confused with the the stand deviation. So never omit the M. from S.E.M.

Did you find the two errors in the paragraph immediately above? If not, look again; then let that be an example to show how carefully one must correct a script.

After you have prepared the first draft of your thesis, read again pages 7 to 26 herein.

If the examiners find faulty logic, they will tell you, even if it is as trivial as 'The patient had anaemia because I observed a low r.b.c. count', or if you imply that the animal body contains serum.

Do not be discouraged

Are you overwhelmed by all the details that need your attention? I hope not. Attending to details takes time, which may prevent your doing all the experiments you would like to do. May I remind you that

> 'A good thesis based on few results
> betters a bad one based on many'?

Even though they point out errors, the examiners are probably sympathetic. They will not fail you for a few small faults if they are convinced that you are a good researcher and that you are able to communicate and, above all, that you can think.

Chapter Eight
Further reading

References

Baer, D. M. (1983). Adjectives, nouns, and hyphens. *Science* **222**, 368.
(1) Booth, V. H. (1960). Legibility of print. *Research* **9**, 2–5.
Clark, G. Kitson (1960). *Guide for Research Students Working on Historical Subjects*. Cambridge University Press.
de Bono, E. (1967). *The Use of Lateral Thinking*. Pelican Books, Harmondsworth, UK.
Dixon, H. B. F (1983). Return of the dalton. *Trends in Biochemical Science* **8**, 49.
Hartree, E. F. (1976). Ethics for authors: a case history of acrosin. *Perspectives in Biology & Medicine* **20**, 82–92.
Hawkins, C. (1982). Write the MD thesis. In *How to Do It*, pp. 52–61. British Medical Association, London. See **8** (7).
Hers, H.-G. (1984). Making science a good read. *Nature* **307**, 205.
Hildebrand, M. (1983). Noun use criticism. *Science* **221**, 698.
Holman, E. (1962). Concerning more effective medical writing. A plea for sobriety, accuracy and brevity in medical writing. *Journal of the American Medical Association* **181**, 245–7.
Kenny, P. (1983). *Public Speaking for Scientists & Engineers*. Hilger, Bristol.
Mackay, A. L. (1977). *Harvest of a Quiet Eye*. Institute of Physics, Bristol.
Maier, N. R. F. (1933). An aspect of human reasoning. *British Journal of Psychology* **24**, 144–55.
Norman, P. (1980). *Sunday Times Magazine* 1980–03–02.
Norris, J. R. (1978). How to give a research talk: notes for inexperienced lecturers. *Biologist* **25**, 68–74.
Perttunen, J. M. (1975). The English sentence. *Luonnon Tutkija* **79**, 113–17.
Roland, C. G. (1976). Thoughts about medical writing. XXXVII. Verify your reference. *Anesthesia & Analgesia . . . Current Researches* **55**, 717–18.
Wolner, K. A. (1975). *Claude Emile Jean-Baptiste Litre, International*

Newsletter for Chemical Education (International Union of Pure & Applied Chemistry), No. **11**, 7–9.

Instructions to authors

(2) Many journals issue Directives to authors. A good example is the *Biochemical Journal's Instructions to Authors*, which includes a piece on Policy, useful lists of abbreviations symbols, etc. and a reminder to write RNAase and DNAase. Obtain the booklet from the Biochemical Society (59 Portland Place, London W1N 3AJ).

If you have not seen a questionnaire that editors send to referees, try to obtain one. Then ensure that your paper would elicit satisfactory answers before you submit it.

Books on scientific writing

(3) Woodford, F. P. (1970). Editor, *Scientific Writing for Graduate Students*, Macmillan, New York & London.

(4) Houp, K. W., & Pearsall, T. E. (1977), in their *Reporting Technical Information*, Glencoe Press, New York, and Collier–Macmillan, London, have an entertaining chapter on writing in clear English.

Scientists Must Write: A Guide to Better Writing for Scientists, Engineers & Students, by Robert Barrass (1983), Chapman & Hall, London, includes a section on reading the literature, which is unusual.

(5) *How to Write and Publish a Scientific Paper*, by Robert A. Day (1988), ISI Press, Philadelphia, and Cambridge University Press, gives a wealth of advice on how so to write that your paper will be accepted for publication.

A Manual of Style, University of Chicago Press, is one of the best-known style books in the USA.

(6) *How to Do It* (1982), British Medical Association, London, is the most versatile of these books. Written by medical doctors, the essays tell how to write, to speak, to chair a conference, to attract a reader, to referee a paper, to be a dictator, to examine, to be examined, to use a library and to perform two dozen other activities.

Science Writing for Beginners, A. D. Farr (1988), Blackwell, Oxford.

Better Scientific & Technical Writing, by M. I. Bolsky (1988), Prentice Hall, New Jersey.

(7) *The Chemist's English*, by Robert Schoenfeld (1985), VCH Verlagsgesellschaft, Weinheim. A book of entertaining essays.

Research: How to Plan, Speak & Write about It. Edited by Clifford Hawkins & Marco Sorgi (1985). Springer-Verlag, Berlin. Eight essays by various writers.

How to Write & Publish Papers in the Medical Sciences, by E. J. Huth (1982), ISI Press, Philadelphia, includes a piece on ethics.

There are other books on science writing, including a version of this book in Japanese, Tokyo, 地 人 書 館 (Chijin Shokan).

English usage

(8)
(9)　H. W. Fowler's *Modern English Usage*, as edited by E. Gowers, Oxford University Press, or by M. Nicholson (as *American–English Usage*, Oxford University Press Inc., New York), is invaluable. The Nicholson edition is out-of-print but well worth seeking.

E. Partridge's *Usage & Abusage: a Guide to Good English* (1982), Hamilton, London, is preferred to Fowler by some editors.

Some passages in each of these books are slowly becoming outmoded.

Everyman's Good English Guide, by Harry Fieldhouse (1982), Dent, London, is more contemporary than the other works, but not so extensive. The book gives help on many troublesome words and recommends pronunciation. The grammatical section is easily readable.

Another helpful book is E. S. C. Weiner's (1983) *The Oxford Guide to English Usage*, Oxford University Press. This book includes a Glossary of troublesome words.

John O. E. Clark's *Word Perfect* (1987), Harrap, London, is a dictionary of current usage. Entries include words that are often confused, errors of grammar and advice on using clichés, vogue words and foreign words.

10)　Strunk, W. (1959). *The Elements of Style* (various editions, e.g. with E. B. White), Macmillan, New York.

11)
12)　*What a Word!* by A. P. Herbert (1935), Methuen, London, who calls you Bobby, shows that good style need not be dull. B. Dixon (1973) in Sciwrite (*Chemistry in Britain* **9**, 70–2) urges lively writing and gives examples of stuffiness.

Books for editors

13)　*Copy-Editing*, third edition, by J. Butcher (1992), Cambridge University Press, contains a great amount of information, some of which cannot easily be found elsewhere. The book describes the astonishing amount and variety of work that has to be done on a script and its illustrations between its receipt by the publisher and touching of the first key by the typesetter. It covers up-to-date methods of book production, including the 'electronic typescript'.

4)　*Editing Scientific Books & Journals*, by Maeve O'Connor (1978), Pitman, Tunbridge Wells, is excellent; every editor should have this book.

The Oxford Dictionary for Writers & Editors, Clarendon Press, Oxford, helps with many problems of detail (capitals, spelling, abbreviations, confusables . . .) that only specialists can remember in total.

The British Standards Institution (2 Park St, London W1A 2BS) has issued various standards of interest to scientists and editors, e.g. BS5261 (1976) on *Copy Marking & Proof Correcting*.

Dictionaries

(15)   *The Concise Oxford Dictionary*, Oxford University Press.
    Chambers Twentieth Century Dictionary, Chambers, Edinburgh.
    The Collins Concise Dictionary of the English Language, London.
    Reader's Digest Universal Dictionary, London.
    The *Oxford* and the *Collins* prefer *-ize* spellings, which are more suitable than *-ise* for international English.

(16)   For American meanings or spellings that are sometimes different from European, consult, for example, *Webster's New Collegiate Dictionary of the English Language*, Merriam, Springfield, MA, or the *Concise Oxford Dictionary*.

(17)   *Roget's Thesaurus* is invaluable in helping one to find a word. Several editions are available. Differently arranged is *Collins New World Thesaurus*, by C. Laird (1979), Collins, London & Glasgow.

    Every scientist should have a dictionary of science. A good one is the *Dictionary of Science & Technology* (1988), Chambers, Edinburgh, and Cambridge University Press.

    There are other science dictionaries. To test one, look up items in your own subject. If the entries are out of date, beware!

    More a book to be read than consulted as a dictionary is *Words of Science*, by Isaac Asimov (1974), Harrap, London.

Units & nomenclature

The source book of units is *Le Système Internationale D'Unites (SI)*, (1985), Bureau International des Poids & Mesures, Sèvres, France. The book contains an English translation. More suitable for the research scientist are the following book and leaflet.

(18)   *Quantitites, Units, & Symbols* by the Symbols Committee (1975), The Royal Society, London.
    Quantities, Units & Symbols in Physical Chemistry, by K. H. Homan, is an abbreviated list published by Blackwell Scientific Publications, Oxford.

    A beautiful chart, *Quantities & SI Units*, is printed in seven colours and published by Nederlands Normalisatie-instituut, Polakweg 5, Rijswijk ZH, Netherlands.

    If you have difficulty in understanding a unit as defined in one book [many of us do], try reading about the unit in a different sort of book, for example a science dictionary.

(19)   BS3763 (1976) on *SI Units* and BS4795 (1972) on *All-Numeric Dates* are issued by The British Standards Institution, 2 Park St, London W1A 2BS.

Rules for nomenclature of chemicals are given in *Nomenclature of Inorganic Chemistry*, by IUPAC (International Union of Pure & Applied Chemistry) (1989), Butterworths, London, and *Nomenclature of Organic Chemistry* (1979), Pergamon, Oxford. Some of the information in the latter is in *Biochemical Nomenclature & Related Documents* (1978), Biochemical Society, London & Colchester, and the price is much lower.

(20)   For a quick check on spelling of chemical names you may consult a well-produced catalogue of chemicals. Such catalogues include *Laboratory Chemicals*, BDH Chemicals Ltd, Poole, Dorset BH12 4NN.

Date of printing

The dates given for the books are the dates of issue. A date may be that of a reprinting of an older edition.

Index

Suffixes *a*, *b*, *c* refer to top, middle and lowest thirds of a page, respectively.